T0069254

INSTITUTE OF CZECH LITERATURE OF THE CAS
KAROLINUM PRESS

CZECH LITERATURE STUDIES

JIŘÍ TRÁVNÍČEK

A Nation of Bookworms?

The Czechs as Readers:
Reading in Times of Civilizational Fatigue

INSTITUTE OF CZECH LITERATURE OF THE CAS
KAROLINUM PRESS

2021

INSTITUTE OF CZECH LITERATURE is part of the Czech Academy of Sciences
Na Florenci 3/1420, 110 00 Prague 1, Czech Republic
www.ucl.cas.cz

KAROLINUM PRESS is a publishing department of Charles University
Ovocný trh 560/5, 116 36 Prague 1, Czech Republic
www.karolinum.cz

This publication originated with the support of the long-term conception
development of the research institution 68378068 and with the support
from the Czech Academy of Sciences.
During the work on this book use was made of the Czech Literary Bibliography
research infrastructure – https://clb.ucl.cas.cz/, (ORJ identifier: 90136).

Cover and graphic design DesignIQ
Set and printed in the Czech Republic by Karolinum Press
First edition

Cataloguing-in-Publication Data is available from the National Library
of the Czech Republic

ISBN 978-80-7658-020-6 (Institute of Czech Literature, CAS)
ISBN 978-80-246-4661-9 (Karolinum Press)
ISBN 978-80-246-4662-6 (pdf)

Contents

Tables and graphs

Illustrations

Matěj Václav Kramerius (bust by Gustav Zoula) (source: author's archive)

Josef Jungmann (portrait by Antonín Machek) (source: https://cs.m.wikipedia.org/wiki/Soubor:Anton%C3%ADn_Machek_-_Portrait_of_Josef_Jungmann.jpg)

Editorial office of the encyclopedia *Ottův slovník naučný* (litography by Josef Roubalík) (source: https://cs.m.wikipedia.org/wiki/Soubor:Redakce_Ottova_slovniku_naucneho_1891_Roubalik.png)

Interwar Czechoslovakia (1930) – map of language distribution (source: https://cs.m.wikipedia.org/wiki/Soubor:Czechoslovakia_1930_linguistic_map_-_created_2008-10-30_ES.svg)

Preparing for the Fučík badge exam (1953) (source: ČTK)

Queueing for books during the Velvet Revolution in 1989 (photo by Josef Chuchma, source: courtesy of Josef Chuchma)

Public library in Otrokovice after the floods in 1997 (source: author's archive)

Neoluxor, largest Czech bookshop (Prague, Václavské náměstí) (source: author's archive)

Book fair in Havlíčkův Brod (source:https://cs.m.wikipedia.org/wiki/Soubor:Book_Fair_2014_Havl%C3%AD%C4%8Dk%C5%AFv_Brod.jpg)

Hans Christian Andersen Night (Albrechtice 2016) (source: author's archive)

National Library of the Czech Republic, originally a Jesuit College called Klementinum (source: author's archive)

Project of the new National library building (architectural visualisation, architect Jan Kaplický, source: http://kaplickycentre.org)
… and all that's left (bus stop in Brno-Lesná) (source: author's
archive)
The most iconic illustration for the most iconic Czech book –
by Adolf Kašpar (source: https://upload.wikimedia.org/wikipedia
/commons/a/a0/Babicka-II.jpg)
Alena Mornštajnová, one of the most widely read Czech authors
today (source: author's archive)
The Egg and I – cover of the first Czech edition in 1947 (source:
author's archive)
The Egg and I – cover of the 6th Czech edition in 1989 (print run:
99 000 copies) (source: author's archive)
The eytracking method, which detects eye movement on the page
(source: https://upload.wikimedia.org/wikipedia/commons/b/be
/Eyetrackingtech.jpg)
Cover of the English edition of Gabriel Zaid's *Los demasiados libros*
(2003)(source: author's archive)

Introduction

Here at the outset there's nothing for it but to start off with some thought-provoking quote. I shall entrust this task to my favourite Jewish-Polish-American prose writer Isaac Bashevis Singer: "Many writers say they write only for themselves. They are hypocrites. If men would stay on an island, all alone, and they knew that nobody would ever publish anything they wrote, they would write nothing. When you write, the reader is always there."

CZECH SELF-STEREOTYPES

There are plenty of nations that describe themselves as "a nation of readers". The Czechs are no exception. It is all part of their mythology about themselves, according to which they are also a nation of musicians, hikers, do-it-yourselfers, gardeners and weekend-cottagers. Combining all these self-stereotypes, we are left with a very Central European *Biedermeier* character, who spends his Saturday digging in the garden at his cottage somewhere by a river and then makes a cup of coffee in the afternoon and sits down in a (home-made) armchair and has a nice read before getting together with a bunch of friends round a camp fire to play guitar and have a sing-song. Yes, this is romanticism, but the homely kind that's nicely under control and not too boisterous. In a word, Central European *Gemütlichkeit.*

STRUCTURE OF THIS BOOK

Although mythology and self-mythology have their unmistakable charm, this book is going to attempt something rather different – to go beyond them and perhaps even against them. Our aim will be to reveal Czech reading culture from the broadest possible perspective. We shall begin on a rather general note with a chapter on reading culture – what it is and what its boundaries are. We will then turn to Czech reading culture, examining it first from a historical perspective and then from a present-day standpoint. This will be followed by a focus upon the domestic discourse on reading and readership over approximately the last 10–15 years and then a quantitative perspective (with statistics from four representative surveys) and a qualitative one (with narrators' depositions and readers' life-stories from research in the 2009–2015 period). The next section aims to present a comparison of Czech reading culture with those of others, on the basis inter alia of statistical data. In conclusion we give the floor to those involved in the creation of everything to do with books and reading and indeed to its co-creators and some of those who reflect upon it. All this is to be brought to a summarizing conclusion in which we would like to reflect the current state of reading culture in general both in this country and elsewhere. Here we shall be asking whether reading nowadays needs some new mission, and if so, what this should be.

ON A RATHER PERSONAL NOTE

The author of this book is by profession a literary scholar. He studied at a time when academic freedoms in his country were being suppressed, and tuition was for the most part contaminated by ideology. That is one reason why at the time he tended towards structuralism – a defensive position of sorts, which also provided the security of firm ground beneath his feet – after all a piece of work such as a language structure is something quite unassailable, though it was perhaps more a case of securing his own position against possible external attacks on works, primarily of an ideological nature. By the late 1980s, before the Communist era had come to an end, this security started to wear thin, as a work cannot merely be legitimized by defending it against whatever it essentially is not. A positive legitimization must also be found. And here the author of this book came to the conclusion that literature is a relational entity, i.e. that its identity only emerges in communication. In other words: every work requires two people – an author and a reader. You cannot have one without the other, as Singer confirms above. In this respect structuralism did not offer any solid ground beneath our feet, as in its view the reader has a really bad reputation – both because he comes from the outside and because at best he presents himself as someone who merely has a duty to implement what the structure of the work has prescribed for him. He has no personal initiative, let alone any context of his own. Moreover, a further uncertainty arose at this point: Are not all the "semantic dramas" involved in poetic and narrative structures, no matter how intellectually clever and captivating they are, rather artificial dramas? Are they not just comfortable speculation from a text-centric ivory tower? After all should we not move on to the dramas offered by communication itself, bringing us much closer to the empirical reader, i.e. seek him out and obtain his testimony directly? And where such testimonies do not exist, at least examine indirect ones, i.e. open ourselves up to the social dimension of literature, which alone provides a view of literature as a whole and in its entirety.

ACKNOWLEDGEMENTS

Here I would like to express my thanks to all those who have given my ideas momentum, valuable inspiration and methodological input: Richard D. Altick (for opening up the field of research into the ordinary reader), Stanisław Jan Bystroń (who mapped out the idea of the literary public, even as a concept, as early as 1938), Robert Darnton (for the flexibility with which he wrote about early modern age phenomena and those created by the digital revolution), Roger Chartier (for his methodological input particularly with regard to historical research into readership), Miha Kovač (for his reflections on the book market), Albert Manguel (for the engaging way he wrote his *A History of Reading*), Anne Mangen (for her thorough, empirically-based research into e-reading), Vít Richter (for always reliably providing the organizational and technical underpinnings for our four joint statistical surveys), Jonathan Rose (for making the connection between social history and the history of reading), Stanisław Siekierski (who considered reading in its cultural context and as a cultural technique that partly supplements standards and partly works against them), Erich Schön (who convincingly considered the turn of the 18th and the 19th centuries to be a great mental watershed period in our civilization, particularly as a result of the proliferation of reading), Shafquat Towheed (for his initiative on the editorial front, as well as in the Reading Experience Database project), Maryanne Wolf (who has made a marvellous connection between neurological findings and the "soft" sciences, while her conception of writing is also an inspiration for personal projects), and there are several others too.

February–June 2020

1
Reading culture

In this chapter we would like to define the term reading culture – what it is and what its boundaries are.[1] It will be useful to look at reading culture from two standpoints – the synchronic (systematic) and the diachronic, particularly in order to avoid the excessively presentistic vision to which our times have succumbed. The digital revolution (and the social and cultural changes it has brought about) is often described from this standpoint alone, particularly with regard to the technical opportunities involved, while audiences (and their reactions) are taken into account far less, and the historical reflections, i.e. their orientation on a time axis, even less.[2]

---

1   This part is based to a large extent on the author's introductory chapters in his book *Kulturní vetřelec. Dějiny čtení – kalendárium* (Brno: Host, 2020).

2   Selected literature on reading culture: Alfred Clemens Baumgärtner (ed.), *Lesen. Ein Handbuch* (Hamburg: Verlag für Buchmarkt-Forschung, 1974), pp. 523–642; Petra Bohnsack – Hans-Friedrich Foltin (eds.), *Lesekultur. Populäre Lesestoffe von Gutenberg bis zum Internet* (Marburg: Universitätsbibliothek, 1999); Janusz Dunin, *Pismo zmienia świat. Czytanie, lektura, czytelnictwo* (Warszawa: Wydawnictwo Naukowe, 1998), pp. 189–197; Anna Dymmel, "Kultura czytelnicza – teoria i praktyka." In Anna Dymmel, – Sebastian Dawid Kotuła – Artur Znajomski (eds.), *Kultura czytelnicza i informacyjna – teoria i praktyka. Wybrane zagadnienia* (Lublin: Wydawnictwo Uniwersytetu Marii Curii-Skłodowskiej, 2015), pp. 9–59; Hartmut Eggert – Christine Garbe, *Literarische Sozialisation* (Stuttgart: J. B. Metzler, 2003), pp. 19 and further; William A. Johnson, *Readers and Reading Culture in the High Roman Empire* (Oxford: Oxford University Press, 2010), pp. 3–16; Rudolf Lesňák, *Horizonty čitateľskej kultúry* (Bratislava: Slovenský spisovateľ, 1991), pp. 10–71; János Riesz – Hans-Walter Schmidt-Hannisa (eds.), *Lesekulturen. Reading Cultures* (Frankfurt am Main: Peter Lang, 2003), pp. 7–12; Gerhard Schmidtchen, *Lesekultur in Deutschland. Ergebnisse repräsentative Buchmarktstudien für den Börseverein des Deutschen Buchhandels* (Frankfurt am Main: Börsenverein des Deutschen Buchhandels, 1968); Erich Schön,

THE CONCEPT OF THE WHOLE

Let us start with a conceptual purge using the *reading as a media skill /
reading as a value system / reading culture* triad. The key term of the first
element is competence (the capacity to read, its practical implemen-
tation and technical skill), the second element involves cultivation of
values (preferences, selection and the ability to interpret and evalu-
ate); and it is only in the light of the third element that we are able to
see both the first and the second within their network of relations and
determinants (keyword: motivation, reason, context). I read because
I am able (*reading as a media skill*), I read because I want to (*reading as
a value system*) and I read because I am part of a particular network of
relations and premises (*reading culture*). Reading culture places reading as a media skill and reading as a value system within appropriate
socio-cultural frameworks and historically underpins them. The reading perspective cannot get by without the writing perspective, but in
sharp contrast the writing perspective need not take account of the
reading perspective. At least that is what we have become accustomed
to. In other words, the perspective of the author and the work only
optionally anticipate a reader – and only when this is recognized as
being appropriate, and for the most part only in the case of a par-
ticipant in literary operation (reviews, polemics and so forth). On
the other hand the reader's perspective (i.e. the reception) contains
within itself both the work and its author, as reading always entails
reading *something*, behind which there is always *someone*. Hence it is
only the reader who makes out a final account of the communication.
This is succinctly expressed by Czech writer Ludvík Vaculík: "I do not
write because of the readers, but it is written for them,"[3] meaning
something like "from the standpoint of the author the reader need not
be present, but from the standpoint of literary communication, the
reader plays an irreplaceable role, which cannot be neglected."

"'Lesekultur' – Einige historische Klärungen." In: Cornelia Rosebrock (ed.), *Lesen
im Medienzeitalter* (Weinheim – München: Juventa, 1995), pp. 137-164.
3   Ludvík Vaculík, *Hodiny klavíru* (Brno: Atlantis, 2007), p. 83.

In other words, each of the three main parties involved in communication (potentially) has something to do with the other two. For example the author is the originator of the text destined for the reader, the text always has its author, as well as its addressee, but it is only when a text is taken up by a reader that we can be sure the communicational potential has become the communicational reality, i.e. that it has been realized and the intention has become the deed. The problem, from the standpoint of history in particular, is how to record the given linguistic potential in its state of communicational reality, i.e. how to clearly allocate it as a social action. We often find ourselves with a lack of evidence, i.e. there are no traces to indicate the behaviour of readers at any given time.

WHO IS INCLUDED IN READING CULTURE?

The internal experience of reading (just like the author's internal experience of writing) remains difficult to detect, so Robert Darnton believes that we should focus our efforts on reconstructing the social context of reading,[4] which according to Polish bibliologist Irena Socha is of a dual nature. The first aspect might be called the *socio-demographic profile* (sex/gender, age, social status, education, place of residence), and the second the *reference community,* comprising our profession, social ties, interests and value preferences.[5] All of this should warn us away from creating some kind of fuzzy reading, as in the example of deconstruction (particularly in the case of Paul de Man),[6] or post-structuralism (in the case of Roland Barthes).[7] There

---

4   Robert Darnton, *The Case for Books. Past, Present, and Future* (New York: Public Affairs, 2009), p. 203.
5   Irena Socha, "Lektura – przekaz, komunikacja czy relacja?" In Anna Żbikowska-Migoń – Marta Skalska Zlat (eds.), *Encyklopedia książki* (Wrocław: Wydawnictwo Uniwersytetu Wrocławskiego, 2017), pp. 99–113.
6   Primarily in the book *Allegories of Reading. Figural Language in Rousseau, Nietzsche, Rilke, and Proust* (New Haven – London: Yale University Press, 1979).
7   Primarily in the book *The Pleasure of the Text*, transl. by Robert Miller (New York: Hill and Wang, 1975 [1973]).

is no such thing, even at the synchronic level, let alone the diachronic level (i.e. from a historical perspective).

Hence if the existence of two social contexts is a constitutive part of reading then we will not be able to do without those who engage as protagonists in the contexts in question, i.e. the readers. A reader is not a voluntaristic usurper of the semantic purity of a text, i.e. its violator. Then again, readers are not just marionettes carrying out the text's instructions. The space that they inhabit might be called *contingent freedom*. This is appositely expressed by Martyn Lyons: readers create their own meanings, but they do not just create them entirely of their own volition. They "are not passive or docile".[8] British cultural historian Jonathan Rose has put it differently, when he sttates that those who examine the historical development of reading are compelled to express "a general dissatisfaction with the Frankfurt School, *marxisant* criticism, all of which tended to treat the ordinary reader as the passive victim of mass culture or capitalism or the discourse of patriarchy".[9]

The question is *who* to include in reading culture. It was previously believed that only those who read serious literature could be included, because only such literature is capable of adopting a non-specialist (i.e. an aesthetic) stance. However, the precarious nature of this definition has become increasingly evident – fiction can also be read quite pragmatically for special-interest purposes, i.e. in order to obtain information (e.g. in historical and war novels); poetry that has been imposed on a school pupil as compulsory reading material thereby goes beyond merely adopting a non-specialist stance. It is an educational tool. A counterpart of this stance is the statement that reading culture ought to just include readers who are known to only turn to reading material in their leisure time and for enjoyment. This

---

8   Martyn Lyons, *A History of Reading and Writing in the Western World* (London: Palgrave Macmillan, 2010), p. 6.

9   Jonathan Rose, "The History of Education as the History of Reading," *History of Education* 3 (2007), nos. 4–5, p. 602; online: https://www.tandfonline.com/doi /abs/10.1080/00467600701496922?journalCode=thed20 [accessed 2020-04-01].

standpoint is just a somewhat broader version of the previous one, but even here the problem arises of whether or not we are actually capable of clearly distinguishing between what we read pragmatically and what we do not. And can this generally be established for all social groups? There are genres that clearly capitalize on the fuzziness of this boundary – such as the historical novel and fictionalized biographies. At the time the statistical surveys were carried out, active participants in reading culture included anyone who met certain set criteria – e.g. if they read a book a year, half year, month, fortnight, week etc). Here we abandon the criteria of *belles lettres* (serious literature) and the character of the reading (in one's leisure time). We should consider all members of the population in question aged six upwards, though we would stress that this only applies to fully literate cultures. Why? Because in communities where reading is a key competence fostered by (compulsory) school attendance, we are *de facto* all readers. Each one of us is dependent upon the written word.

READING CULTURES

Statistics and qualitative findings clearly confirm that there is a women's reading culture and a men's reading culture, which differ from each other fundamentally, primarily in the intensity of the reading (which is higher for women) and perhaps also in their appreciation of fiction (which is again higher for women). They also confirm that they differ in their age cohort – e.g. in the present-day Czech population (and elsewhere), reading decreases significantly in middle age. It also differs in terms of reference communities – so that IT middle managers read one thing in one way, while humanities lecturers at universities or grammar school pupils read something else in a different way. Each community of this kind takes something different for granted, and in terms of reading culture, a network of different texts is involved. In other words, the prerequisites of group identity are by and large not transferable outside the group in question.

There are also certain national formulas involved here which have been created historically and culturally – for example, in terms of the number of books read per year the level for the entire Czech population corresponds to the level of people with higher education aged 40+ in the Polish population. The Scandinavian countries have a far better-developed approach to public libraries, while they do not have such a sharp division between "highbrow" and "lowbrow" literature. Hence it is more likely for them to review detective stories in their dailies and magazines, just as it is for them to espouse such literature, as it does not bear such a social stigma. The proliferation of e-books among Americans is considerably greater than it is in Western Europe, while the United Kingdom acts as a kind of intermediate zone between the two cultures. Europe itself is largely under the sway of a north-south polarity, with the highest reading rates in Scandinavia and the lowest in the south (e.g. Portugal, Greece and Malta). In Canada there is a large difference between Anglophone and Francophone cultures – with the former standing out for its much higher reading rate. There again in Israel a difference arises between various types of Jewish immigrants, with the strongest reading group comprising immigrants from Europe and old established settlers (*Yishuv*). In Hungary (as in Poland) there is a great contrast in reading habits between the urban and the rural populations. In the USA books are bought mostly by older people, while in the Czech Republic mostly by the middle-aged. Research has even been carried out into the "cultural honesty" of individual nations, i.e. how (un)willingly they admit that they have not read particular books, especially those in the canon. The French came out worst while the Americans fared best.[10] This reveals another variable in any particular culture: a kind of reading snobbery coefficient.

One way or another a pluralistic conception of reading culture (i.e. as reading cultures) provides a good safeguard both from above and

---

10   See Heinz Steinberg, "Books and readers as subject of research in Europe and America," *International Social Science Journal* 24 (1972), no. 4, pp. 744-755.

below. From above against "astral" theorizing, which in its search for general concepts becomes blind to all time-contingent variables, and from below against psychologizing "show me a reader and I'll show you uniquely autonomous reading within its own cultural ecosystem" relativism. Moreover, this pluralistic conception enables us to a far greater extent to see reading culture in all its historical variability.

FROM A HISTORICAL STANDPOINT

Reading culture can only enjoy prestige and influence as a social reality if a sufficient number of participants (users) are engaged in it. At a worldwide level the majority of the population did not start to be literate until the 1950s. As for Western civilization (which was foremost in associating its cultural identity with reading and books), this took place at the turn of the 19th century. Although culture does not involve parliamentary elections, even here it is the case that only a majority can claim any cultural dominance, and it is only in this situation that reading becomes more than just a bonus that privileges its adherents. The reverse is also the case, and those who have not espoused reading find themselves in a cultural deficit and a state of social exclusion.

If we systematically apply a sociocultural approach then the entire history of reading culture can be divided into two halves: from approximately 3500 BCE to the turn of the 19th century and then from the turn of the 19th century to the present day – while we must emphasize that this only applies to Western civilization and not to the world as a whole. The age of majority illiteracy, when orality (oral transmission) was the primary way in which information was passed on, and the age of majority literacy, when orality was edged out by the written word. It is only in these contexts that we can mark out the more subtle boundary lines, particularly with the help of technological changes (primarily typefaces, text fixation methods and forms and reproduction and distribution techniques). The following scheme indicates that even in a written culture the great majority of the human population have spent most of historical time in an oral culture.

READING CULTURE AGE	INDIVIDUAL PERIODS (OF CULTURE)	HISTORICAL EPOCHS
Dominance of orality Circa 3500 BCE - turn of the 19th century	The oldest written culture: Mesopotamian cultures; cuneiform, usage for technical purposes - counting units for stocktaking, contracts of purchase; the very narrow circle of those associated with writing, their extreme exclusivity.	Antiquity
	The culture of esoteric sanctity: writing acquires a sacramental role - ancient Egypt; writing provides access to occult (esoteric) knowledge; the narrow circle of priests and scribes who enjoy exclusive status.	
	The culture of the founding texts (*Gilgamesh*, Homer's *Iliad* and *Odyssey* epics and the oldest part of the Hebrew Bible): these are strong cultural and religious identity reference points; writing as a tool to record people's internal states and stories; emancipation from utilitarian and sacramental functions; a still very narrow circle of readers, even though they are no longer just sporadic circles of initiates; this method was developed by the ancient (especially Hellenic) world; thanks to the simplification of writing (with the emergence of an alphabet) the literacy threshold is brought down.	
	Codex culture: the codex greatly facilitates reading and reduces the reliance upon professional readers brought about by scrolls; various reading environments are created - religious, aristocratic and royal courts and burghers, but reading does not occur outside these circles.	Middle Ages
	The culture behind the emerging mass output of books: the invention (or rediscovery) of typography, which becomes the principal means by which books are made more easily available; the increasing role of the burghers and their participation in reading; the great differences between the town and the country; the overall expansion of literacy.	Early Modern Age
	Reading culture as a mission of emancipation: the Enlightenment; reading as a source of individual freedom and thus also of progress and sociocultural independence; readers as cultivators of a critical attitude to the world; faith in educational and cultural institutions.	

Predominance of writing	The culture of the great watershed (end of the 18th century): a sharp rise in literacy, a change in the book market structure, a new relationship between the author and the reader as a result of book market changes – the emergence of the reading public; a transition from intensive reading (repeated reading of just a few titles) to extensive reading (one-off reading of many titles); reading mania, reading hunger; reading as a threat – political, social and health; the great role played by reading in the emergence of modern-day national identities.	The long 19th century
Turn of the 19th century – present (early 21st century)		
	The culture of bourgeois hegemony: latter half of the 19th century: predominance of the bourgeoisie, for whom reading becomes a kind of secular religion; the first period in which reading begins to noticeably compete against itself: books versus magazines, pulp fiction versus challenging literature; the golden age of the book.	
	A culture in which reading loses its media monopoly: first half of the 20th century; reading in competition with new media – film and radio; first indications of mass fashions (the bestseller phenomenon), which means the end of the predominance of the bourgeoisie as the primary culture-creating power; sobering down from the Enlightenment ideal that the extent of literacy indicates the extent of progress and civilizational well-being.	The short 20th century
	The culture of predominating visuality: latter half of the 20th century; expansion of television; the entire world definitively tilts over onto the side of literacy; significant increase in output; television as a big competitor, particularly because it offers comfortable participation in visual culture at home; the question arises whether we are not witnessing the twilight of reading culture.	
	Computer and digital culture: the technological leap forwards, thanks in particular to new media (computers and the internet); easy availability of everything, which also entails the phenomenon of overabundance; fragmentarization of reading culture; another wave of lamentation over the end of reading culture; the multimedia and transmedia reader; coronavirus crisis – a huge threat to the book market, closure of libraries, shared reading on social networks.	End of the 20th and beginning of the 21st century

WHAT NEXT?

These digital times have on the one hand exacerbated the opposition between focused reading and superficial reading, while on the other hand the internet itself is now an expansion of the Gutenberg galaxy. The boundary line has also hardened considerably between the professional and the public spheres. Never before have there been so many opportunities to access reading material and information on books and writers. Likewise there have never been so many opportunities to acquire books (both legally and illegally), and there have never been so many traces left behind by readers (blogs, discussions, Facebook reading communities, opinion polls and so forth). Moreover, the statistical data indicate there is a visible correlation between readers and internauts.

Is the digital age going to destroy reading culture? It does not look that way so far. At the moment all we know for sure is that it has considerably expanded its horizons. However, what is certain is that the digital age is substantially transforming reading culture. Just how intense this transformation is going to be, where it will lead, where it will all end, what it will involve and what its (technical, cultural and neurophysiological) nature will be remains an open question.

SUMMARY AND CONCLUSIONS

Reading culture is a broad concept, a concept with rather permeable boundaries, and a historically variable concept to boot. Moreover, we must remain aware of its two dimensions – the narrower (receptive) aspect and the broader (communicative inclusive) whole. This applies to everything involving writing and to a lesser extent language. The words *reading* and *culture* seem to support each other if not actually overlap, as culture may be considered to be anything that is shared (read), and not just produced (written). Indeed it is only here that we can speak of culture in the true sense. In other words, culture represents the circulation, scope, extent and ecosystem of relations and all that is related.

However, the perspective of the whole, no matter how complete it may be from the communication standpoint, is fragile in a way, because the counterparty (the reader) often only provides a limited number of direct testimonies. Hence reading culture is a culture of the literate, but to a large extent it is also the culture of the mute. However, this does not mean that it is invisible and cannot be observed, although it can often only be observed indirectly – primarily from the social circumstances surrounding reading.

Reading culture involves the rule of three i's. Its *i*nclusivity, i.e. its ability to encompass a broad set of various phenomena, is primarily possible thanks to the *i*mplicit nature of its boundaries (and their permeability), which thus creates a model that is to a large extent *i*ntuitive.

2

From a historical standpoint

In this chapter we would like to present Czech reading culture from a historical standpoint, particularly from the first stirrings of the National Revival in the late 18th century.[11] This is a time that is often characterized – within the context of Western civilization – as the reading revolution,[12] referring to the transition from intensive reading (the recurrent reading of just a few titles) to extensive reading (one-off reading of many titles), which is associated with the strictures of the book market in the present-day sense and the emergence of public libraries. It was a time when reading had ceased to be a social privilege and was now increasingly a civilizing duty. We shall also take into account the determination and modification of the three basic reading patterns established during this period: *patriotic, bourgeois* and *transmedial.*

---

11   For a brief history of Czech books see Devana Pavlik, "The History of the Book in the Czech Republic and Slovakia," In Michael F. Suarez – H. R. Woudhuysen (eds.), *The Book. A Global History* (Oxford: Oxford University Press, 2013), pp. 461–469.

12   See Asa Briggs – Peter Burke, *A Social History of the Media. From Gutenberg to the Internet* (Cambridge: Polity Press, 2005), particularly p. 53; Guglielmo Cavallo – Roger Chartier (eds.), *A History of Reading in the West*, transl. by Lydia G. Cochrane (Amherst – Boston: University of Massachusetts Press, 2003 [1997]), pp. 284–312; Rolf Engelsing, "Die Perioden der Lesergeschichte in der Neuzeit: Das statistische Ausmass und die soziokulturelle Bedeutung der Lektüre," *Archiv für Geschichte des Buchwesens* 10 (1970), pp. 944–1002; Martyn Lyons, *Books. A Living History* (London: Thames & Hudson, 2013 [2011]), p. 9; Jonathan Rose, "The History of Education as the History of Reading," *History of Education* 3 (2007), nos. 4–5, p. 599–604; Erich Schön, *Der Verlust der Sinnlichkeit oder Die Verwandlungen des Lesers. Mentalitätswandel um 1800* (Stuttgart: Klett-Cotta, 1987).

UP TO THE END OF THE 18th CENTURY

However, the history of Czech literary culture (and with it reader-ship) does not just begin at the end of the 18th century. The first literary manuscripts found on the territory of the historical lands of Bohemia and Moravia are texts written in Old Slavonic from the 9th century, originating with Cyril and Methodius, the two missionaries from Thessalonica (and later saints), who were invited to Great Moravia to establish a writing system there and translate some of the Bible into it, as well as some key liturgical texts. Old Slavonic was subsequently ousted by Latin. However, the 13th century saw the emergence of Czech, which gradually developed into a fully-fledged language capable of presenting an ever broader range of functions and genres. From this time on until the end of the 18th century Czech literary culture (and literary life) goes through several peaks, troughs and periods of stagnation. The peaks include the reign of the Luxembourg King Charles IV (1346–1378), who made sure the original Old Slavonic culture was maintained. Czech literary culture also flourished during Hussite and post-Hussite periods (in the 15th century), even though the former was notable not only for the development of literature but also for the destruction of books and their sale abroad. Another heyday was the "Veleslavín" period at the end of the 16th century, which is notable for its broad range of genres and interests, while one of the most important Bible translations (the Kralice Bible) was also written at that time. This came to be the standard on which the modern Czech language was based at the beginning of the modern era.

As for the reader background it is possible to find more or less the same trends in the Czech lands as in other Western cultures. In the Middle Ages reading is widespread particularly in ecclesiastical and aristocratic circles. In the early modern age we can see the slow emergence of the bourgeoisie and the associated laicization of the reading repertoire. In both cases there is a huge difference between the town and the country, while information and tradition are primarily borne by oral culture, while written culture only operates to a very limited extent. Reading (as literacy and cultural practice) is understood to be a cultural benefit, not a civilizing necessity. Also to be taken into consideration is the unavailability of books, both financially and otherwise, which did not basically change as printed books came onto the scene from the latter half of the 15th century.

NATIONAL REVIVAL (TURN OF THE 19th CENTURY – MID-19th CENTURY)

The Czech cultural situation at the end of the 18th century was in some respects the same as in the neighbouring countries, but in other respects quite different. It was the same to the extent that it, too, was affected by the Enlightenment and the reforms promoted by the Habsburg sovereigns (Marie Theresa and Joseph II), but different in that these Enlightenment reforms lacked any Czech upper echelons.

At this time Czech was the language of the countryside and the less affluent urban population – occasionally ridiculed by the local German inhabitants as the "language of the housemaids". When following the Battle of the White Mountain (1620) the Evangelical nobility (the majority of Czechs being Evangelical at this time) were forced to emigrate, the Czech lands were transformed in three ways – (1) as a result of anti-Evangelical repressions and the Thirty Years War (1618–1648) the country lost one third of its population; (2) there was re-Catholization (which was anti-Evangelical, but not anti-Czech); (3) German came to be the dominant language. It should be added that the Czech lands were part of the Austrian Empire from 1526, but it was only the period following 1620 that saw an increase in repression and the curtailment of many rights.

This state of affairs continued more or less until the end of the 18th century, although it should be mentioned that the Baroque period, which preceded the Enlightenment, did not bring about any decline

Matěj Václav
Kramerius
(bust by
Gustav Zoula)

in culture here. Moreover, the Jesuit order (the dominant power during the Baroque era) was of an essentially missionary character and so endeavoured to maintain Czech amongst the broadest social strata. In other words, although many later interpreters called it a "dark" age, i.e. a period of decline, it definitely did not involve any cultural or literary downturn (as numerous excellent works were created in all fields of art, Czech Baroque came to be a phenomenon of European importance particularly in sculpture and visual art). As for the language, we might refer to a decline in its standard version, as there was a lack of a generally respected written (literary) standard of Czech: hence the language was in a very unstable state, and a binding standard needed to be established. This need was also felt in other cultures, e.g. Serbian, Croatian, Slovenian, Bulgarian, Greek and Slovak.[13]

As regards Czech national interests, the Enlightenment was a highly contradictory project. On the one hand it improved literacy figures, thanks in particular to the introduction of compulsory school attendance (1774), but then on the other hand in its Habsburg form, this meant strong centralization, which went hand in hand with Germanization. Paradoxically, the rapid development of the Czech-speaking people from below came up against state Germanization from above, as German was meant to become the sole official language of the Habsburg Empire. In any case, in contrast to France, where it was born, the Enlightenment in the Habsburg Empire came from above; the priority was an efficient state and not the individual and his or her national requirements.

As Czech society gradually emancipated itself from German influence, it created the institutions of national culture, science, scholarship and education for itself. A key element in all this was literacy. When compulsory school attendance was introduced into the Czech lands (in 1774) there were 1,109 "trivial schools",[14] but the following year their number had doubled and by 1847 tripled. That year 93% of boys (of school attendance age) went to school and 91% of girls.[15]

Czech was limited (in Czech-speaking areas) to trivial schools, which children had to attend from the age of six to twelve. Outside this area (and the home) it was only kept alive by the clergy and ecclesiastical circles, particularly for pastoral purposes – without Czech the priests would have become alienated from the ordinary people.[16] A knowledge of German was essential for entrance to sec-

---

13 See Peter Burke, *Languages and Communication in Early Modern Europe* (Cambridge: Cambridge University Press, 2004), pp. 89-110.

14 These were rural schools providing primary education in the "trivium", i.e. reading, writing and arithmetic, both for boys and girls.

15 See Zdeněk Šimeček - Jiří Trávníček, *Knihy kupovati... Dějiny knižního trhu v českých zemích* (Praha: Academia, 2014), p. 118.

16 See Miroslav Hroch, *Na prahu národní existence. Touha a skutečnost* (Praha: Mladá fronta, 1999), pp. 54-58.

ondary school. The rapidly expanding circles of the literate had to be accommodated by publishing literature written in Czech, and at the same time these circles had to be encouraged and incentivized. A pioneer in this field was Matěj Václav Kramerius, whose publishing activities (at the *Česká expedice* publishing house) endeavoured to accomplish several objectives at the same time – to express respect for old Czech literature (by publishing heritage documents), to publish periodicals in an attempt to reach a broader public, and tireless promotional activity, thus attempting to combine the ideals of the Enlightenment with zeal for the national cause. He must have dealt with a rather narrow circle of readers, who were not too affluent, so they could not afford to buy his books and periodicals.

As for the nature of the reading matter, the lower classes (those in rural areas and craftsmen) were to a large extent reliant upon religious writings (generally catechisms and prayer books). Almanacs enjoyed great popularity. These were works that offered advice to farmers, prayers, stories, recipes and so forth. The more educated public read primarily in German. At this time original Czech fiction and didactic literature was gradually emerging, as were translations from foreign literatures. The intensive reading method still predominated. Despite the significant growth in literacy and the expansion of the range on offer, its momentum was still great, and the extensive reading method was only slowly taking over. Within the context of extensive reading, however, a patriotic reading pattern was also emerging, primarily as a project from above, its proponents being the very sparse Czech intelligentsia and bourgeoisie. The Enlightenment mission, which in major Western cultures (British, French and to a large extent German) is associated with reading, is filtered in the Czech environment through the national emancipation mission. In other words, being an educated, aware citizen and being a conscious proponent of Czech language and culture (and thus also a reader of Czech books) largely came to be synonymous.

LATTER HALF OF THE 19th CENTURY

The latter half of the 19th century set new tasks for Czech society, as the Czech language was successfully revived, providing a binding standard (thanks to Josef Dobrovský), as well as creating basic reference works (particularly Josef Jungmann's *Czech-German Dictionary*), thus awakening Czech nationalism, the basic features of which were anti-German sentiment and Slavism. However, the latter gradually began to wane in strength, thanks in part to certain Czech writers' and thinkers' personal experience of Russia (journalist and poet Karel Havlíček described this disillusion most stingingly). What was known as Austro-Slavism came into being, i.e. the idea that Czech culture's

Josef Jungmann
(portrait by
Antonín Machek)

"home" location was Central Europe, as the Habsburg Empire would form far more suitable conditions for such coexistence, particularly by federalizing.

How did the Czechs at this time stand in comparison with other nations in the Habsburg Empire? Much better off than the Slovaks, who were fewer in number and lacked a network of national organizations, but considerably worse off than the Hungarians, who were increasingly conscious that they were a dominant nation within the Empire along with the Austrian Germans, as became fully evident in what is known as the Settlement (*Ausgleich*) in 1867, when Austria became Austro-Hungary. Moreover, the Hungarians were exerting pressure on the other small Pannonian nations, i.e. the Slovaks, Romanians and Croats. The role of the Poles was quite unique, as they lived in three areas of occupation (Prussian, Russian and Austrian), with the Austrians being by far the most moderate, thus providing a refuge for numerous activities (including publishing) and for people, particularly from the Russian area of occupation.

Whereas Czech was successfully defended during the first half of the century as a language producing serious (as well as educational) literature, the task during the latter half of the century was to make sure there were readers for this literature. In the first case this particularly meant creating a bourgeoisie and in the second case the emancipation of the Czech book market from the German. Both markets were then taking shape, but only very slowly and not without difficulties.[17] As regards Czech literature, it was only in the 1860s (and then increasingly in the 1870s and 1880s) that it attempted to move beyond national-patriotic tasks.

The requirement to read Czech books was borne not only of patriotic desires or the need for entertainment. The fact that this mission was somewhat ahead of readers' needs and desires is borne out by the many complaints made by Czech writers that their books were

---

17   See Jan Thon, *Osvětou k svobodě. Kniha o českých čtenářích* (Praha: Aventinum, 1948), pp. 109-147.

Editorial office of the encyclopedia *Ottův slovník naučný* (lithography by Josef Roubalík)

not selling, that there was a lack of discerning readers and that the readers preferred entertaining reading, if not downright trash. There was also no lack of complaints over the scant support for Czech authors and Czech books. The Czech book market is truly very small, and it is not possible to make a living just from writing books for Czech readers, as was discovered by Božena Němcová, the greatest Czech woman writer of the 19th century, who died in 1862 in great material need surrounded by slander and gossip. In 1881 and 1885 two manifestos were brought out in support of the Czech readership and Czech books, with an appeal for support for municipal libraries, as well as for the bourgeoisie to not be so lacklustre towards Czech books and not least, for nationalist agitation against foreign books: "Anyone who prefers books and magazines from the foreign, aye the enemy side, to our own books is not one of us.".[18]

The Czech patriotic model predominated, and within that framework – as a subtype – popular reading, plus to a somewhat lesser extent – as a second subtype – the reading of national classics. The

18 Ibid., pp. 138–147.

setting is primarily rural. Almanacs were read, as were religious tracts and titles that were primarily entertaining, which the technical progress of the 19th century helped to publish in far larger print-runs for much lower prices. However, the bourgeois model also began to emerge at this time, focusing more on reading as a programme of individual development, as well as the aesthetic distinctiveness of literature. Elsewhere in the world (particularly in France) this was a time of emerging modernism, which placed such requirements at the fore.

FIRST REPUBLIC (1918–1938)

The Versailles Treaty created several successor states out of Austro-Hungary, one of which was Czechoslovakia, a country with 13 million inhabitants and many nationalities. In 1921 Czech nationality was claimed by 6.84 million inhabitants, while 3.2 million registered as German, 1.98 million as Slovak, and 0.65 million as Hungarian, while there were also many of Ukrainian/Ruthenian and Polish ethnicity. The official doctrine was "Czechoslovakism", whereby the Czechs and Slovaks were considered to be a single nation with two branches; the first Czechoslovak constitution (of 1920) begins with the words "We the Czechoslovak nation…" The idea behind Czechoslovakism was primarily meant to help the Slovaks, so that they did not become the third largest nation in the Republic. Likewise with regard to literacy, this was an extremely disparate area: the Czech lands (Bohemia, Moravia and Czech Silesia) were almost 100% literate, while there was 15% illiteracy in Slovakia and 52% illiteracy in Sub-Carpathian Ruthenia. As for the number of books published, at the end of the First Republic period these came to almost four-fifths (78.9%) in the "Czechoslovak" language (69% in Czech and 9.7% in Slovak), while approximately every seventh book (14.8%) was published in German and every fortieth (2.5%) was in Hungarian. French was the most frequently represented foreign language with 1.2% of domestic output.

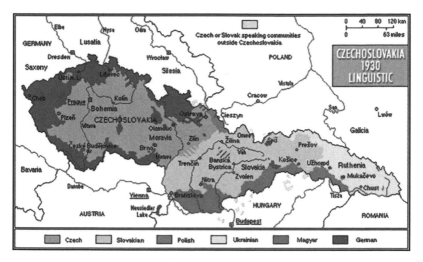

Linguistic map of interwar Czechoslovakia (1930)

Reading culture expanded enormously in Czechoslovakia thanks to the opportunities afforded by the period in question (even though each of its parts had a different dynamic) and extended to its fullest in the Czech lands. Many new publishing houses were established, and the book market began to develop in a far more systematic way. In 1919 a Public Libraries Act was passed, stipulating that every constituency had an obligation to set up and maintain a public library and setting out the administrative rules, as well as the type of literature to be handled. "Writings that are worthless artistically or in terms of their content, works of an immoral nature (i.e. pornography), 'penny dreadfuls', detective and cowboy stories that inflame the reader's imagination with sensationalism, pamphlets which tendentiously demean entire classes and strata of the population, as well as works targeting the existence and integrity of the Czechoslovak state may not be included in public libraries."[19]

---

19 *Zákon o veřejných knihovnách obecních č. 430/1919 Sb. a navazující předpisy;* online: https://ipk.nkp.cz/docs/legislativa/KnihovniZakon_1919.doc [accessed 2020-03-31].

As regards patterns of reading, the most common of these re-mained the patriotic kind (together with both of its subtypes: popular reading and national classics). However, the bourgeois pattern had also been successfully and fully developed. According to public library loans and the answers in various surveys, here we can distinguish two subtypes: entertaining reading and more challenging works. The latter is represented primarily by such foreign authors as John Galsworthy, Sinclair Lewis, Erich Maria Remarque and Edgar Wallace.

Numerous discussions also took place over why the more challenging works did not enjoy the reception that their authors and literary critics expected. At the same time opinions were voiced that the publication of valueless literature should be curtailed so as to save paper. Some of these reproaches were being levelled at the writers themselves, even from amongst their own ranks – e.g. that Czech literature lacked political novels, as well as books from modern-day life (Josef Hora). The Czech author writes without really knowing anything (Pavel Eisner); The Czech novel easily falls under the sway of modernist experiments, thus losing its attractiveness for readers (Benjamin Klička).

SECOND WORLD WAR (1939–1945)

After the dismemberment (or de facto dissolution) of Czechoslovakia following the Munich Pact (30.9.1938), German aggression continued, the rump of the country was occupied on 15 March 1939 and the Protectorate of Bohemia and Moravia was established. This involved a de facto occupation and hence the subordination of Czech culture to German administration. Although the Czech lands did not see as much administrative violence and victimization during this period as Poland, it was in fact fighting for the very existence of its national culture. Strict censorship was brought in with lists regularly compiled of proscribed titles. Books themselves were also censored, sometimes in a rather comical fashion – hence the term "Polish soup" was banned from cookbooks. Before a book was accepted, its author had to present proof that he was not a Jew.

The number of books published was greatly reduced and strict censorship set in, so space primarily opened up for the publication of classics. Publishers and booksellers came up with the slogan: "Read Czech books". For example Božena Němcová's *Babička* (Granny), the most iconic work in all Czech literature, was published 29 times in 1940 alone. Interest also increased in poetry, particularly Czech. Individual poetry collections were brought out in unprecedented print-runs. The entire Protectorate can be seen as a period of recoil, so that again it is primarily the patriotic reading pattern that comes to the fore and as part of this the reading of national classics. Hence the purchase and loan of Czech books came to be a small token of quiet resistance and patriotism. Books were now a scarce commodity, and huge sums of money were paid for them on the black market. This was also because they were unrestricted goods, i.e. they did not require rationing coupons.[20]

UNDER THE COMMUNISTS (1948–1989)

Following three years of limited postwar democracy (1945–1948), the Communists took power in a coup, plunging the entire country into the sphere of Soviet influence, and making Czechoslovakia a political and economic satellite of the Soviet Union, just like the other countries of Central and Eastern Europe.

As far as reading culture was concerned, the first phase was marked by its ideological activism. Private publishers and bookshops were closed down and strict censorship was reintroduced. As for public libraries, at one time they were being considered to take on the role of distribution points in lieu of the book market, which was considered to be a remnant of capitalism. Later this system was abandoned, just as the centrally-managed book market system was. In 1961

20　See Zdeněk Šimeček – Jiří Trávníček, *Knihy kupovati...*, p. 298.

administrative and economic autonomy was introduced among lower administrattive units (regions). The Communist regime was attempting to present itself as the party most concerned over the education of all strata of society, as well as the one fighting hangovers from the old times (particularly trash literature), but this was all being done from above, primarily through regularization. The reader could only choose from what was permitted. Hundreds of authors and titles were prohibited and thus deselected from library collections in two waves (in the early 1950s and the early 1970s).

This endeavour to manage and channel reading was most evident during the 1950s (under Stalinism).[21] The most vociferous campaign was called the "Fučík badge", named after Communist journalist Julius Fučík, the most iconic hero of that period, who was executed in 1943. The Fučík badge came into existence back in 1949, when it was published in an instructional publication *Jak získám Fučíkův odznak?* (How do I get a Fučík badge?). This campaign primarily targeted youngsters. Contenders were meant to select the required number of books from various items (political books, progressive fiction, books of poetry, Soviet novels and specialist literature to match the contender's profession) and then read them. After reading them they were to go before a commission, where they were examined to see if they had correctly understood the books. The test ended with a song, after which the contender received a Fučík badge, whose holders were called *fučíkovci* (Fučíkers), and those who wore it were considered to be a political elite of sorts, as being one of them cleared the path to a brighter career both at school and the workplace. While the Fučík badge was used in a positive campaign for a "new reader", there was no lack of negative campaigns against trash literature, Western literature, decadent (read Western) literature and so forth. Likewise they campaigned against detective stories, which – according to the

---

21   See Roar Lishaugen, "Incompatible Reading Cultures: Czech Common Readers and the Soviet Mass Reader Concept of the Early 1950s", *Scando-Slavica* 21 (2014), no. 1 (60), pp. 108-127.

Exam preparation for the Fučík Badge (1953)

leading representative of domestic librarianship at that time, Jaroslav Frey – were supposed to be "literary works that were alien to the Slavs", particularly because the "Slavs' solution to crime is cleansing and liberating," while the problem of crime in the capitalist world is a "criminal-technical matter".[22] Individual reading was also consid-

---

22   Jaroslav Frey, "Práce se čtenářem," *Knihovna* 3 (1948), p. 94.

ered to be a bourgeois relic, as the collective was supposed to take pride of place.

One particular reading culture phenomenon came to be known as "Book Thursdays", particularly during the 1970s and 1980s. There was one particular distribution day (Thursday) when new book titles were sold at the bookshops. Long queues formed from early morning in front of the bookshops for books in demand (though not all of them), particularly titles by several Czech writers who had for a time been forbidden (e.g. Bohumil Hrabal and Vladimír Páral), Anglo-American detective novels (Raymond Chandler, Agatha Christie and Ed McBain) and world bestsellers (e.g. Arthur Hailey, Mario Puzo and Mario Simmel).

The ruling régime's projects entitled "New Reader" and "Socialist Reader" (cf. the socialist reading pattern) did not succeed, as people were guided more by their own personal taste, and many of them by what had been prohibited. To a large extent they utilized their own private libraries, which actually served as educational institutes of a sort. During this period it was the bourgeois pattern that was by far the most developed – i.e. reading as an autonomous programme and to a large extent an escape from official indoctrination. The regime could only chalk up individual successes within the patriotic pattern – attempting to "rewrite" some of the classics (e.g. by Alois Jirásek, the author of historical epics) for its own purposes, interpreting their patriotism as a key to social progress, and turning Jirásek, and particularly his image of Hussitism, into a precursor of Marxist-Leninist ideology.

At the same time some of the campaigns introduced by the Communist regime played a positive role in spite of the ever-present ideology involved, as its representatives considered themselves to be civilizing modernisers, which also meant that they were fostering public education, an important part of which was reading culture. In 1955, March was designated Book Month, which led to its promotion as such and to the support of reading culture in general (by means of various events such as exhibitions, readings, bookshop window displays and forums). An effort was made to present books in the remotest parts of the country, as well as at factories and farms. Book clubs also had a high organizational and dramaturgical standard, particularly the Young Readers' Club, whose distribution network was made up of primary schools.

The Communist period was also a time when Czech literature (and the entire book world) was divided into three different areas – officially published output, unofficially published output (*samizdat*) and output in exile,[23] involving different systems of distribution and reception. Unofficially published literature operated clandestinely, the main form of transmission being from hand to hand, occasionally through postboxes. Publications were duplicated on typewriters (with an original plus twelve copies), and it was only at the end of the 1980s that computer printers started to be used. The circle of readers was rather narrow, basically encompassing the intelligentsia, students and only sometimes workers too. They were in general read hastily overnight from one day to the next (following the "read and pass on" instruction), and the speed with which these books circulated was high. Output in exile could be found mainly in Czech émigré communities (e.g. in the USA, Canada and West Germany) and was distributed by post. An effort was also made to illegally infiltrate it to the greatest possible extent into Czechoslovakia, where circulation expanded thanks to serial transcription.[24] The state threatened various penalties for owning this literature and especially for copying it – from academic expulsion and dismissal from employment to imprisonment.

---

23   See e.g. Miha Kovač, *Never Mind the Web. Here Comes the Book* (Oxford: Chandos Publishing, 2008), pp. 146-153.

24   See Michal Přibáň and co., *Český literární samizdat 1949-1989. Edice, časopisy, sborníky* (Praha: Academia-Institute of Czech Literature, CAS, 2018), particularly pp. 13-87.

POST-1989

The social and political changes brought about by the Velvet Revolution were quickly reflected in reading culture and the book realm and were evident even to the naked eye. The publication of a book interview with Václav Havel, *Dálkový výslech* (Long-distance Interrogation) was a downright heroic act that was accomplished within several weeks, a quite unprecedented amount of time. When Václav Havel was elected President (29 December 1989), the book was already in circulation. Let us not forget that under the Communists there was nothing exceptional about a book even taking three years to come out – from submission of the manuscript to review, composition and printing.

The book market and everything to do with books underwent a very rapid *liberalization*, which lasted until about the mid-1990s, as the old state monopoly system for publishing and selling books slowly began to collapse. New publishing houses mushroomed, while the old ones revised their publishing programmes. Books were being sold everywhere possible (e.g. in kiosks and from street stalls) and there was great interest in them – particularly those which had been banned under the old regime.[25]

The next phase was the *transformation*, which can be pinned down to late 1991. Publishing continued at a frenetic pace, while many books were evidently turning out to be unsellable as the old system wound down. The first signs of a surplus crisis began to show. Many of the old publishers had to radically change their business practices.

The third phase was *stabilization*. This lasted for a long time until around 2013, definitively confirming that the state of affairs just prior to 1989 would never recur. Book print-runs were radically reduced and there was no longer a name, topic or genre to attract the same

---

25   See Jan Halada, *Encyklopedie českých nakladatelství 1949-2006* (Praha: Libri, 2007), pp. 15-17; Jiřina Šmejkalová, *Cold War Books in the 'Other' Europe and What Came After* (Leiden - Boston: Brill, 2011), pp. 333-365.

Queueing for books during the Velvet Revolution in 1989
(photo by Josef Chuchma)

Public library in Otrokovice after the 1997 floods

attention as before. Complaints were made about Czech readers – to the effect that they were not such book lovers as they appeared to be. Many publishers refused to take account of this new situation, stubbornly clinging to the notion that enthusiasm and a firm idea of what makes a book good were all it took to deal in books. However, most of them went under. There was now even talk of authors being silenced again, this time "by economic factors".[26] It was not until now that publishers and booksellers were finally willing to change their strategy from "a good book always finds its readers", which they had got used to from the old regime and the first years after 1989 to

26 See Milan Nápravník, "O sounáležitosti surrealisty," interview by Irena Zítková, *Nové knihy* 33 (1994), no. 9, p. 9; Andrew Wachtel, *Remaining Relevant after Communism. The Role of the Writer in Eastern Europe* (Chicago: The University of Chicago Press, 2006), pp. 44-97.

"a book has to chase its readers". This process was also significantly affected by the digital revolution – with new options emerging for information acquisition, book distribution and even the form taken by books (and other reading material).

The final phase is *integration*, i.e. the period from 2013 to the present day. On the book market this has taken the form of the acquisition and accumulation of capital – the bigger are beginning to get even bigger and just a few large distribution companies are gaining ground, while the smaller ones are disappearing. Likewise bookstore chains are gradually starting to appear, as are companies combining wholesale and retail with publishing.

As for the reading pattern, the patriotic version in particular is still hanging in there (particularly among the older generation), while since 1989 several authors (mostly female) of popular literature, which the previous regime dismissed as debased, have again been successfully published. On the whole the bourgeois pattern is also holding on, even though here too the lower level – i.e. the bestsellers – can be seen to be getting stronger. All the big hits got into readers' hands in a very short time, and to a large extent they responded positively. However, a new reading pattern then evolved – the transmedial. This primarily applies to the younger (and the youngest) generation. It is the result of the digital revolution, even though its first traces can be found as far back as the 1930s, when film and radio first started to develop. Hence it is not entirely the case that young people have moved over from printed to digital media. It is only a new distribution of roles that has emerged. And even if the printed book (especially fiction) is still more important than, for example, the e-book, the boundaries between individual media and forms of books (printed books, e-books and audiobooks) are understood to a large extent to be fuzzy – which is a state matching Bauman's *liquidity*[27] and Jenkins' *convergence*.[28]

---

27 Zygmunt Bauman, *Liquid Modernity* (Cambridge: Polity Press, 2000).
28 Henry Jenkins, *Convergence Culture. Where Old and New Media Collide*

Neoluxor, the largest Czech bookshop (Prague, Wenceslas Square)

THE CORONAVIRUS CRISIS (2020)

The declaration of a state of emergency in mid-March 2020[29] meant the closure of schools, public institutions (including libraries), shops (except foodstores, drugstores and chemists), services and factories. This came together with a broader range of electronic sources on offer, with celebrities reciting texts and making them available for public sharing. The social networks were flooded with requests for people to buy books direct from the publishers (at their e-shops). Recommendations abounded in books on great epidemics such as Camus' *The Plague*, Defoe's *Diary of a Plague Year* and *Love in the Time of Cholera* by García Márquez. As people had to restrict their movements

---

(New York – London: New York University Press, 2006).
29   It lasted until 17 May 2020 – the first phase; the second phase has lasted from 27 December until now (April 2021).

outdoors to a minimum, they felt compelled to stay at home and thus to read more, to read to others and to share their reading tips and recommendations, and because the public libraries were closed they were more reliant upon their own domestic resources, e-books and online bookshops. The social networks also saw the arrival of some ludic forms, e.g. a chain relay of recommendations, in which every day someone is challenged to put up a list of favourite books on his or her Facebook wall (without any assessments) and at the same time as each recommendation is made to challenge somebody else to do likewise and to challenge someone else and so forth. For many people this results in an inspiring reading list.

Book fair in Havlíčkův Brod

SUMMARY AND CONCLUSIONS

The first Czechoslovak President Tomáš Garrigue Masaryk, himself a great reader and a man who put a lot of thought into his reading, called the Czechs a "philological nation". Indeed the Czechs based their modern-era existence (in contrast to the Poles and the Hungarians, but perhaps like the Slovaks, Finns, Ukrainians and Norwegians) on language and thus indirectly on books and reading, and over two centuries of modern-era existence they have more or less confirmed this trait. For the Czechs reading has become something of a secular religion, indeed a religion that is quite widespread. Although the Czech Republic does not boast a reading culture that is quite as extensive and institutionally well-catered-for as in the Scandinavian countries, reading there is a far more widespread activity than in other Central European countries. For example the number of those who read at least one book a year is over twice that of Poland.

Here we view reading as a form of national emancipation (in the National Revival) and then as individual emancipation (in the latter half of the 19th century and during the First Republic), reading as a basic survival programme (under the Protectorate), reading as a broadly based cultural alternative and an enclave for intellectual liberty (under the Communists), reading as a cultural given (during times of satiety and civilizational fatigue), which lacks a strong and socially acceptable cultural mission (post-1989).

3
From the present-day standpoint

In this chapter we shall be looking at the current state of Czech reading culture, focusing attention in particular on such institutional pillars as the book market, public libraries and state policy, as well as campaigns in support of reading. We shall also be taking an interest in the current state of affairs that has come about, and just how it came about.

THE BOOK MARKET

The current state of affairs on the Czech book market can be summed up as on the whole satisfactory. There is an extensive range on offer, which is well-structured. This means that it provides space both for the mainstream (for the "majority" reader) and for various reading minorities and subcultures. Let us first look at the publishing dynamics in terms of the number of titles published.[30]

If we compare recent information with data from the Communist era (during the 1980s) the increase in the number of titles is fourfold, while this table clearly shows the political watershed. Between 1990 and 1995, output rose twofold. These were the years when the Czech book market underwent a radical transformation in all respects. The rise in the number of fiction books during this time (almost threefold) due to the relaxation in the previous censorship is also striking, as it was primarily fiction which had been most suppressed and which was thus under the greatest pressure to be published. Since

---

30 According to the ISBN register; this is the figure sent to UNESCO.

Table 3.1 Titles published 1990-2019

	1990	1995	2000	2005	2010	2015	2017	2019
number of titles published	4,136	8,994	11,965	15,350	17,054	18,282	16,422	17,330
of which, fiction	13%	36%	27%	22%	26%	29%	30%	30%
number of titles per thousand inhabitants	0.4	0.9	1.2	1.5	1.6	1.7	1.6	1.7

Source: National Information and Advisory Centre for Culture (NIPOS)

2005 the number of published titles has more or less stabilized at the present-day level, in the case of fiction at around 25%. The record year to date was 2011 (with 18,985 titles).

Focusing on the range of this output in terms of original works versus translations, the translated titles come to around 35%, of which rather more than one half are translated from English. The other languages involved are German (with around 15% of translated titles), Slovak and French (about 5.5%) and Russian (about 3.5%). French and German have done significantly worse than they did under the First Republic (1918–1938) and Russian has done worse than it did under the Communists (1948–1989). For example, in 1981 almost twice as many translations from Russian came out than those from English, whereas in 2017 there were sixteen times fewer.[31] Under the Communists, Russian and the languages of the Soviet bloc enjoyed considerable state support, so they were published regardless of the book market and the interests of readers, who boycotted such books, including, unfortunately, even very high quality works from the perestroika period in the latter half of the 1980s.

---

31   See Michael Wögerbauer – Petr Píša – Petr Šámal – Pavel Janáček and co., *V obecném zájmu. Cenzura a sociální regulace literatury v moderní české kultuře 1749-2014. Svazek II (1938-2014)* (Praha: Academia - Institute of Czech Literature, CAS), p. 1431.

Slovak deserves a special mention, thanks in particular to the many years of history the Slovaks have shared with the Czechs in a common state (1918–1938 and 1945–1992). Most of the population of the Czech Republic at the time knew it as the second federative language.[32] However, for the youngest generation (below about 35) it has become an impediment. The relationship between the two is quite asymmetrical, as even the youngest generation of Slovaks have far less difficulty with Czech than the Czechs have with Slovak, largely because tens of thousands of Slovaks study and work in the Czech Republic.[33] In other words the very publication of a novel in Slovak would be an impediment to the Czech reader due to the language, and hence it would also be a risk for a translator, because for a large proportion of the population, particularly those who are older and more educated, reading a Slovak book in Czech translation is something that would not occur to them.

The e-book and audio-book segments have been expanding dynamically of late here, in contrast to the USA and the United Kingdom for example, where over the last five years or so they have been stagnating and indeed contracting. However, in spite of this growth, their sales have by no means achieved vertiginous heights – with only around 2% of the total of all books sold. A larger proportion (5–10%) is made up of sales to foreign customers, particularly in Slovakia. Audio-book sales have also recently been rising year-on-year, although their share of the total is by no means momentous either – 56% are physical sales and 44% digital sales.[34]

As for total Czech book market turnover, over the last few years we have noted a gradual increase, from around 7.2 billion CZK

---

32 Czechoslovakia was a federation from 1968, when the Constitutional Act on the Federation was passed.
33 According to Czech Statistics Bureau annual data, there were 116, 817 of them living in the Czech Republic in 2018, which is more than one fifth of all foreigners; See https://www.czso.cz/documents/10180/61196236/29002718.pdf/571c5d12 -3744-4d32-a8e2-e1a0f3f30e28?version=1.2 [accessed 2020-04-02].
34 See Zpráva o českém knižním trhu 2018/2019; online: https://www.sckn.cz/file /wysiwyg/files/Zprava_o_ceskem_kniznim_trhu_2018_19.pdf[accessed2020-04-02].

(282 million EUR) in 2013 to around 8.3 billion CZK (325 million EUR) in 2018. Sales of e-books and audio-books make up barely 3% of this volume. According to Association of Czech Booksellers and Publishers information, the number of books that are imported (i.e. that are not published in the Czech Republic) is three and a half times higher than the number of those exported (particularly to Slovakia).[35]

Let us now consider publishing geography. The post-1989 period saw a huge relaxation in the centralism of the publishing world, with an increase in opportunities for publishing beyond the main centre(s) (i.e. Prague and major cities). Over the last few years the situation has stabilized, with slightly more than every second title published in Prague and approximately every eighth book published in Brno.

In geographical terms, the Czech book market is distinctly Prago-centric, though it should be stressed that whereas at present half of all book titles are published in Prague, under the Communists it was three quarters. However, in stark contrast to the pre-1989 period, Brno, the second largest city, has rather grown in importance. Otherwise the trend towards further decentralization that was visible in the early 1990s has come to a halt over about the last fifteen years, and if anything we can now see the publishing centres of Prague and Brno have slightly increased in strength, primarily because the largest publishing houses are located there. The only market segment where the smaller cities are making gains is higher education. The post-1989 period has seen the rise of many new universities in cities with a population of around a hundred thousand (e.g. České Budějovice, Hradec Králové, Liberec and Ústí nad Labem). Of the twenty largest Czech publishers in 2018, fourteen were in Prague and three were in Brno. These are publishers that meet the criterion of a large enterprise (within the Czech context) within this field publishing at least one hundred titles a year.

In the Czech Republic there are 500–550 bricks-and-mortar bookshops, 200 of which are part of bookstore chains. A precise figure

---

35   Ibid., p. 6.

Map 3.1 Published titles by location (2016)

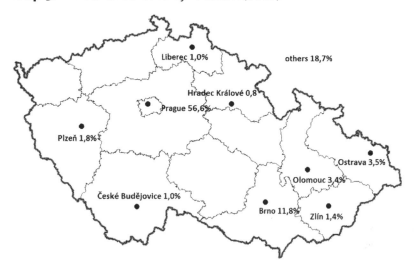

Source: Association of Czech Booksellers and Publishers

cannot be given, because some of the smaller bookshops have to offer a range of other goods besides books. *Zpráva o českém knižním trhu 2017/2018* (Report on the Czech Book Market 2017/2018) states that "there has been a rapid drop in the number of independent booksellers", while "this trend has not been successfully halted". The frequent reason for this is that booksellers retire and often cannot find anyone to carry on the business independently.[36] When a bookshop disappears from a smaller town it is sad in terms of trying to maintain awareness of books and reading. It is even sadder if that bookshop is the only one there.

In the Czech environment the *small extent of integration* is still considered to be a problem. Some movement in this direction has now taken place, but it is thought to be too little, too late. In 2012 the range of titles on offer by the five largest publishers came to 12% of all output. In 2018 it was 18%. At the same time warning voices have

---

36   Ibid., p. 3.

been raised against excessive integration, which might be to the detriment of variety. Hence Albatros Media, the biggest of the Czech publishing giants, has acquired numerous smaller brands, but when incorporating them it has reduced their publishing plans, only taking on what suited it.

The *university and academic market* has been a thorn in the flesh over the long-term – as it lacks a more long-term strategy, a more attractive range of titles and an ability to attract a broader public, while distribution is totally neglected. In order to basically satisfy the needs of those who work at the universities, who only need to get their career texts out there, these publishers often bring them out without any stylistic editing and with only formal peer reviewing. In such circumstances what kind of window dressing can then be done? Moreover, these publishers have seen the rise of that modern-age plague, also often assisted by the grant system, namely collections of conference papers. Without good reason, books have been brought out successfully, but with content "dramaturgy" that is rather problematical, and no one is too concerned about them. In other words, this sphere suffers from a certain asymmetry. The publishers should be the ones seeking a balance between authors and readers, but the university publishers have pushed the centre of gravity far more towards the authors, often merely to satisfy their pragmatic needs. And this is all that lies behind a lot of publications. There has clearly been little editing work behind these published texts, i.e. they have not been thought through or followed through at all. Far more of those which have piled up in editorial offices are published than public interest actually warrants.

There is also a problem regarding the disappearing bookshops, particularly in small cities and towns, and the decreasing number of second-hand bookshops, while another issue is the glut, whereby the "shelf life" of books has been reduced. The Czech reader is overwhelmed by the excessive supply and the market is overheating. This has been made evident, for example, in research focusing on the book market in 2013. Those who had not purchased a book over the previous year were asked why they had not done so. There were almost seven times as many who had not done so because there were too many books on the market than those who had not done so for the opposite reason, because there were too few books.

HOW WE BEHAVE ON THE BOOK MARKET

In the last survey (2018), somewhat less than one half (46%) of the Czech population aged 15+ stated they had bought at least one book per year. On average each had bought 2.6 books per year, spending 646 CZK (25.3 EUR) on them. User behaviour among the Czech population is fairly conservative, as indicated in the following graph.

Graph 3.1   Where we buy books (2018)[37]

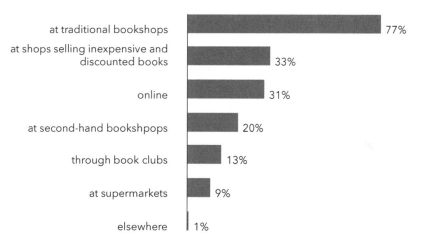

Source: The Czech National Library and the CAS Institute for Czech Literature (Base: those who buy books)

---

37   Total ≠ 100%, because it was possible to answer more than once (up to a maximum of three).

As for socio-demographic characteristics, traditional bookshops are preferred by women, the elderly and those with the highest education, while shops selling inexpensive books are preferred by people from lower income groups and those who have not passed their school-leaving examination, while these also, perhaps surprisingly, prefer second-hand bookshops, again along with those from lower income groups. As for book clubs, here the eldest predominate, while in contrast online purchases are the domain of the youngest, men and those with the highest education.

As regards genres, contemporary fiction, primarily for relaxation (detective stories, current bestsellers and romances), is most popular, while non-fiction (biographies and history) has been doing quite

Graph 3.2   Why we do not buy books (2013)[38]

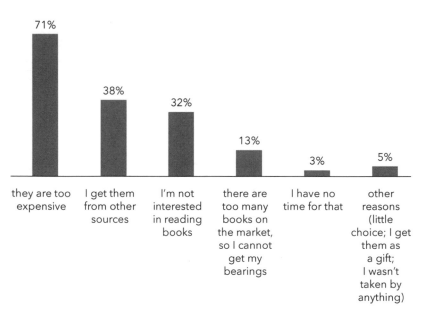

Source: Czech National Library and Institute of Czech Literature, CAS
(Base: those who do not buy books)

---

38   Total ≠ 100% as up to two answers were possible.

well of late, and interest in children's literature has also been notably on the rise.

Let us now look at that segment of the Czech population that does not buy books. What are their reasons and the impediments involved?

The primary status of financial restraints is only to be expected, as is the order of the next two items. However, a comparison of the following two main reasons is far more noteworthy: "There are too many books on the market for me to get my bearings" and "the choice on the market is too small." The ratio here is 13% to 2%, which indicates that almost seven times as many do not make a purchase because of the glut on the market as because of any lack – i.e. the oversaturation syndrome.

IN TIMES OF CORONAVIRUS (2020)

When a state of emergency was declared (13 March 2020), all the shops were closed down except those selling foodstuffs, chemists' goods and a few others, hence all the bricks-and-mortar bookshops ceased operating. The already rather fraught situation on the book market, with some of the wholesalers withholding payments from the publishers, deteriorated further, thus threatening publishers, print-ers, editors, translators and other professions associated with book production and distribution with uncertainties over their income. Several initiatives were thought up to implement a direct sales model between publishers and bookshops to successfully bypass some of the parasitical e-shops that were trying to take advantage of this sit-uation by undercutting book prices (with discounts of up to 80%).

The large players wrote a letter to Prime Minister Andrej Babiš requesting the government to resolve this situation one way or an-other, as otherwise the book market could have entirely collapsed. "Although the book market cannot compare with other branches of industry in terms of employee numbers or economic strength, the social damage of such a collapse would be hard to put a figure on."[39] The main difficulty was that cashflow had almost come to a standstill, so that publishers had lapsed into secondary insolvency, e.g. because they were not receiveing any money from the distributors they had to stop paying their employees (such as editors and graphic artists), as well as the translators, printers and authors. As publisher Barbora Baronová said: "The book market collapsed like dominoes."[40] It was clear that the consequences of the crisis would be long-term, as was stressed by Host publishing house director Tomáš Reichel: "It will take us several years to get back to the previous level."[41] However, one positive element was perceived to be the reduction in the number of published books, which had been too large for the Czech book market.

Several proposals were put forward to help the book market. Writer and publisher Markéta Hejkalová suggested that the state could reduce the salaries of state employees by 10–15% to shore up the booksellers, publishers and other self-employed workers who were most affected by the crisis. The state could also re-open the bookshops, if only for just a few hours, which would also help people in quarantine. The state might also abolish VAT on books, either temporarily or permanently, "and endeavour to massively support the purchase of books from small publishers for public libraries and schools".[42] In an announcement made on 7th April, the Association

39 "Nakladatelé žádají Babiše o pomoc. Varují před likvidací knižního trhu"; *iDNES* (25. 3. 2020); online: https://www.idnes.cz/kultura/literatura/nakladatele -knizni-trh-vyzva-premier-andrej-babis.A200325_112029_literatura_kiz [accessed 2020-04-02].
40 Barbora Baronová, "Knižní trh se zhroutil jako domino," interview by Petr Vizina (**podcast**, 8. 4. 2020); online: https://magazin.aktualne.cz/kultura/literatura/pocast -petra-viziny-knizni-trh-se-zhroutil-jako-domino-rika/r~eadd9b78791d11ea9d470 cc47ab5f122/ [accessed 2020-04-08].
41 Cited from Daniel Konrád, "Zaorálek hodil knižní trh přes palubu, tvrdí knihkupci. Luxor bez pomoci neotevře," (9. 4. 2020); online: https://magazin. aktualne.cz/kultura/literatura/zaoralek-hodil-knizni-trh-pres-palubu-knihkupectvi-luxor/r~cad156fe7a6111ea8b230cc47ab5f122/ [accessed 2020-04-09].
42 Markéta Hejkalová, "Malí a velcí srdcaři", *H7O* (2. 4. 2020); online: http:// www.h7o.cz/den/ctvrtek/ [accessed 2020-04-02].

of Czech Booksellers and Publishers, a professional organization, stated that the annual book market turnover could fall by one third, as could the number of titles published, while at least one third of this amount was being requested of the government as a kind of rescue plan for the entire sphere. The situation slowly began to return to normal at the end of April, when the bookshops were permitted to open again on condition they adhered to strict security measures.

The coronavirus revealed numerous weaknesses in the Czech book market: its fragility, i.e. its meagre resistance to unforeseeable situations and its very weak payment discipline – at the beginning of the crisis one of the largest distributors announced that it was suspending payments (for books received) to third parties. Tensions were also revealed between the big players and the smaller ones, involving their various interests and positions. The crisis also revealed that the professional organization (The Association of Czech Booksellers and Publishers) did not play a terribly strong role, as it does not have any effective tools to enforce discipline over payments and the like. In any case this situation may also be considered to be an opportunity to totally overhaul the Czech book market.

PUBLIC LIBRARIES

Public libraries have been one of the mainstays of Czech reading culture, particularly since the days of the ground-breaking Libraries Act of 1919 (see p. 37). At present the Czech Republic can boast the densest network of libraries in the world, with 5.1 public libraries per 10,000 inhabitants, whereas within the European Union the average is 1.3. In terms of expenditure, however, the situation is quite different: the sum of 15 EUR per inhabitant is expended on public library activity in the Czech Republic, whereas the equivalent amount in Denmark, for example, is 65 EUR. In other words, the network is dense, but at the same time it is a network of relatively impoverished libraries. As is the case in other countries, public libraries are increasingly turning into community and social centres, while the results of surveys into their main services continue to indicate that the Czech population still associate them primarily with books and book loans.

Under an Act passed in 2001, the library system in the Czech Republic comprises (see also Appendix 10):
(1) libraries established by the Czech Ministry of Culture (National Library, Moravian Library and the K. E. Macan Library and Printing House for the Blind);
(2) regional libraries established by the appropriate regional body (totalling 13);
(3) basic libraries established by the appropriate municipal body or another organizer (these form the core of the Czech libraries system);
(4) specialized libraries (museum, medical etc.).

The number of libraries and their users since 1990 shown here.

Table 3.2   Czech public libraries 1990–2019

	1990	1995	2000	2005	2010	2015	2017	2019
number of public libraries	5,838	6,179	6,019	5,920	5,415	5,354	5,339	5,307
number of registered readers per thousand inhaibtants	181	139	148	150	137	134	131	129
number of visitors per thousand inhabitants	1,468	1,390	1,771	2,003	2,107	2,241	2,111	2,067

Source: National Information and Advisory Centre for Culture

As can be seen from the table, the number of registered readers is falling, while the number of visitors over the long term is rising. In other words, we are going to the library more frequently, but no longer as a place to borrow (printed) books. The range of other services is expanding, both in virtual space (catalogues and the inter-library loans service) and on the library premises themselves (educational programmes, forums, authorial readings, exhibitions, workshops and so forth). Around one million people have taken part in such events of late.

Libraries are substantially more frequented by women, the better educated and the young (aged 15–24 years); the number of people of lower social status has also increased over recent times. As regards life cycles, the opposite rules apply to those of the book market, where we buy considerably more in our middle age, whereas we go to the library more in our youth and old age.

As for employment categories, in recent times some three quarters of library staff have been made up of specialist librarians, while the remainder comprise service occupations, most being information and communication technology staff. Which age categories are involved? We have noted a gradual increase in age – in comparison with the 1990s the number of employees aged 61+ has risen twofold, whereas those in the 51–60 age bracket come to almost one third, while in the 1990s they came to one quarter.[43] This is predominantly a female profession – with women making up 87% of the staff and men 13%, while during the 1990s they only made up 7%.

In addition to the aforementioned underfunding, providing a suitable modern building for the National Library is a considerable local issue. Its construction was meant to begin in 2007 based on a design by architect Jan Kaplický, a Czech émigré living in the United Kingdom, but the project was suspended due to a series of administrative interventions and ultimately abandoned (for more details see p. 71). The operation of the National Library on the current premises of the Baroque Klementinum complex in Prague has increasingly proved to be unsuitable both from a technical standpoint and from the users' point

---

43　See Vít Richter – Vladana Pillerová, *Analýza věkové, vzdělanostní a mzdové struktury pracovníků knihoven v ČR 2016/2017. Zpráva z průzkumu* (Praha: National Library, 2017); online: https://www.vkol.cz/uploads/page/171/doc /analyza-vzdelavani-zprava-2017-def.pdf [accessed 2020-04-02].

of view. Moreover, this building also has to contend with another two problems – ongoing long-term reconstruction and a lack of space. This situation does not look as if it is going to be resolved any time soon.

PUBLIC LIBRARY ATTENDANCE

The number of visitors is gradually decreasing, as indicated by the following graph:

Graph 3.3 Public library attendance then and now (2007, 2010, 2013, 2018)

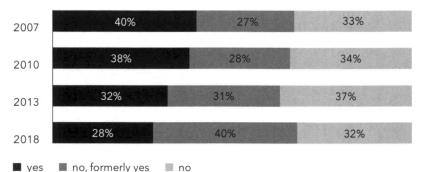

■ yes   ■ no, formerly yes   ■ no

Source: Czech National Library and Institute of Czech Literature, CAS
(Base: entire population)

One trend – a drop in the number of visitors – has carried on, while another trend – an increase in the number of those who have never been to a library – came to a halt. On the other hand there has been a significant increase in the number of those who have been to libraries, where there is a realistic hope that they will go back, generally as seniors.

Which public library services are those who go to them most interested in? These are shown in the following graph. For each service a choice is shown between "use" and "don't use" (with the remainder up to 100%).

Graph 3.4 Public library services (2018)

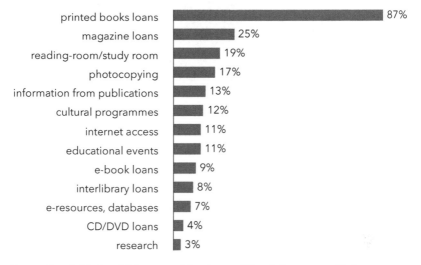

printed books loans	87%
magazine loans	25%
reading-room/study room	19%
photocopying	17%
information from publications	13%
cultural programmes	12%
internet access	11%
educational events	11%
e-book loans	9%
interlibrary loans	8%
e-resources, databases	7%
CD/DVD loans	4%
research	3%

Source: Czech National Library and Institute of Czech Literature, CAS
(Base: those who have visited a public library over the last year)

Book loans remain the primary service – there has been no change in that over the last four surveys, while magazine loans have substantially decreased, as has photocopying. On the other hand cultural programmes and educational events have increased in number, thus indicating – in line with trends elsewhere – the direction that public libraries have now taken. This direction also entails broader cultural openness and a bolstering of the range on offer that is not directly associated with core library activities.

A survey of what is actually loaned will also be of relevance. Over the last few years this has included J. K. Rowling's Harry Potter saga and the latest hits on the Czech book market, as well as school reading. Book loans are shown in the following graph in chronological terms.

Graph 3.5 Loans based on year of publication (2017)

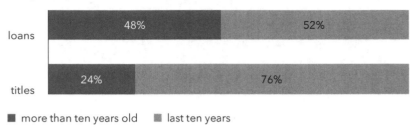

■ more than ten years old   ■ last ten years

Source: Czech National Library

Here we see the emergence of a very prominent presentism, which stands out even more in the case of the second item – loans. It is only these which present the true reality of what actually circulates among readers, and it is here that we clearly see the problem which public libraries have to face – the tension between acquisition needs (to satisfy the demand for popular titles as much as possible) and the cultural role (the ability to offer the broadest possible range from the widest possible timeframe).

The *coronavirus crisis* period (spring 2020) is yet to be dealt with. Under a government regulation the public libraries remained closed and so had to switch to a different mode of operation. They started to provide much greater access to their digitized collections, particularly those which had previously not been accessible outside their own institution. There was an increase in the number of loaned e-books, which had hitherto not been a service that readers used all that much. Following an agreement with Dilia, the collective copyright administrator, the Czech National Library provided students in higher education with access to over 206,000 monograph and periodical titles – but only for reading, not for downloading or printing. This also applies to works protected by the Copyright Act.

OTHER EVENTS AND STATE SUPPORT

Clearly the most prestigious event in all Czech book and reading culture is the World of Books trade fair, which takes place in May each year. It endeavours to maintain a balance between its commercial and cultural programmes, while combining domestic interests with the presentation of guests from abroad. Each annual fair focuses upon a particular national literature or area, e.g. in 2019 it was Latin America. The fair has been taking place since 1995, with the participation of around 400 exhibitors, and in recent years it has been visited by some 40,000 people (see Appendix 9). As far as the first criterion is concerned, it is some seventeen times smaller than the book fair in Frankfurt am Main, which is considered to be the largest and most prestigious undertaking of its kind. As far as the second criterion is concerned, it is around seven times smaller.

The second trade fair (operating since 1991) is organized in Havlíčkův Brod every autumn. It is attended by around 160 exhibitors and visited by some 16,000 people. There are other trade fairs too, but these are much smaller and generally focus on some specialist area.

Thus a pattern which we know from other countries has also established itself here – spring and autumn fairs: one main trade fair and a secondary one, which is nonetheless still socially prestigious. Additionally there are other small trade fairs, which for the most part focus on some particular area of publishing.

State support for reading and readership is very hit-and-miss and lacks any kind of long-term vision, since it is handled in a project-management spirit rather than in terms of policy. Although the state (in the form of the Ministry of Culture) provides some funding (public competitions) for readership-related campaigns, it is not able over the long term to accommodate the requests made by people from this milieu for it to allocate specific financial capital for this area. Hence readership projects compete for funding with literary festivals and competitions, authors' readings and so forth, amongst which they are perceived as something of a Cinderella. A request made by several leading representatives of various associations and spheres (e.g. education, science, public libraries and the book market) in 2016 to have this situation dealt with and above all to establish something like a national programme in support of reading remained unanswered, as introductory negotiations did not lead anywhere. The ministries concerned – of culture and education – were unable to even link up with each other over this, on the grounds that it was administratively difficult. Hence this endeavour has come up against another obstacle – departmentalism.

If anything positive has happened in this area, it has done so thanks to the ideas of private institutions and ardent enthusiasts. Since 2006, for example, we have seen the Every Czech Reads to Kids initiative, an idea that originally emerged in Poland, which endeavours to support reading out loud with the slogan: "Reading to children at least twenty minutes a day". The woman behind the entire project is Ewa Katrušáková, and the range of activities is not only focused on publicity support, but every year a Week of Reading to Children is organized with readings in hospitals and "Grandma and Granddad at Nursery School". Another campaign is Growing Up with Books, a campaign organized by the Association of Czech Booksellers and Publishers, which endeavours to encourage reading through consultations (book tips) and various games and competitions, to inspire the establishment of reading clubs at primary schools, to collaborate with public libraries, to present reading by means of an interactive website and so forth. Since 2017 the professional association of Czech librarians (SKIP) has organized a project entitled Bookstart, which has been operating in 20 countries now for over 25 years. This project involves giving the parents of new-born babies a gift in the form of a set containing a book and methodological instructions on how and what to read to one's child, as well as a library card.

We have much to thank the public libraries for, particularly with regard to reading among children, as they organize numerous special events. Moreover, one Czech "invention" has been the Night with Hans Christian Andersen, an event that first took place in 2000. It was thought up by two librarians from Uherské Hradiště, and has

Hans Christian Andersen Night (Albrechtice 2016)

traditionally taken place ever since around the Danish fairy-tale writer's birthday (2 April), which is also International Children's Book Day. Children are allowed to come into the library and spend the night there, with an extensive programme (readings, competitions and games) laid on for them. This campaign has recently expanded to many other countries. In 2019 there were sleep-overs in 21 countries, with 1,775 sleeping spaces and 98,853 participants, making up a total of almost one million participants overall. Events put on by the

Czech librarians' professional association (The Association of Library and Information Professionals of the Czech Republic) should also be recalled: March – Month of Readers, which has been taking place since 2010, its aim being to ascertain just who goes to libraries and who does not, and in the latter case why they do not and what needs to be done to bring them in. This event ties in with March – Book Month, which was first launched under the old regime (in 1955).

SUMMARY AND CONCLUSIONS

The two institutional mainstays of Czech reading culture (the book market and public libraries) are quite reliable in their operation. Over the last few years the book market seems to have been living in the expectation that some fundamental transformation, i.e. something really major, was due to take place. So far this has been happening more by means of slow evolution and gradual steps, even if many of the processes involved have been accelerated by the coronavirus, and not in an entirely positive way.

Public libraries have been the pride of Czech reading culture over many years, particularly with their dense network. Although we can observe a gradual decline in the number of physical visitors, the number of those communicating with them online is actually increasing.

Things are worse when it comes to the well-planned organization of Czech reading culture at a state level. It can be stated quite unequivocally that in this respect the state is failing or proving to be inflexible and not very perceptive regarding initiatives from below. This is not so much a matter of it being primarily an investor as a coordinator or guarantor. In the role of the one meant to be in charge of ongoing sustainable readership – as is the case in many other countries – it is behaving passively. If it is to actually operate in this sphere then it is more thanks to private initiatives.

4
From the standpoint of discourse on reading culture

Let us now focus on the presence of reading culture in Czech public discourse – i.e. the ways it is spoken and written about, how it makes the greatest impression and in particular how it has stood out beyond its own confines. Let us also narrow down our timeframe to approximately the last ten to fifteen years and note right from the outset that its presence in public debate is neither very conspicuous nor very durable, but this should perhaps come as no surprise, as this is an area that serves as home to some extremely tranquil cultural waters. Politicization and ideologization only occur occasionally during periods of cultural warfare.

THE OCTOPUS

Evidently the only open cultural war with a strongly politicized subtext has been the one that raged around the construction of the new National Library, partly because the first two Presidents of the Czech Republic were involved.

In 2004 Prague representatives were consulted over the new library design, which they approved. In 2005 the construction also received the support of the Czech Lower House of Parliament. The following year saw the announcement of an international architectural competition, which was won by a project designed by a Czech architect (living in exile) Jan Kaplický, based on a study by Future Systems (UK).

National Library of the Czech Republic. Originally a Jesuit College, it is also known as the Klementinum.

Soon afterwards, however, a dispute broke out over just how fair the competition was: twenty Czech and foreign architects sent a public letter to the Minister of Culture, criticizing the alleged bias towards the future winner, as well as the irregularity of the competition as a whole. The plots of land in Letná, Prague, on which the library was due to be built, also came to be a crisis point. Although the Prague town hall had approved the transfer of the land in 2006, it turned out that this decision was not fully binding in law.

A tussle eventually broke out among the legal experts, who were unable to agree on whether the competition had been fair or not. In 2008 the ruling on the competition announcement was suspended and Kaplický himself entered the legal fray. That same year the Czech

Minister of Culture announced that the National Library project would not go ahead after all. National Library Director Vlastimil Ježek referred the matter to the Ombudsman, accusing Prague Mayor Pavel Bém of frustrating the project – first there was enthusiasm and a promise, but then all the agreements were broken. Then President Václav Klaus got involved too, announcing in 2007 that he would prevent the construction "in that form" – with his own body[44]. This bitter cultural tragedy was played out to its ironic end: in 2011 they finally managed to put up the building on a reduced scale as a bus stop on the Lesná housing estate in Brno. Somebody later placed a small bookcase inside it, but this was subsequently vandalized.

Attempts to revive this project were made by the Prague Town Hall under its new management in 2010. Several political parties also came back to the project during election campaigns in 2014 and 2018. Another revival took place in 2019, when the widow of Kaplický (the architect, who had died in 2009) signed a memorandum with the National Library and the Ministry of Culture on the transfer of the copyright. The last wave of interest passed over in the summer of 2019 as a new Minister of Culture took office. In terms of media attention, however, this was a rather marginal event.

The building, whose shape had been etched into popular awareness as the *Octopus* or the *Blob*, has been at the forefront of public debate ever since 2006, along with attacks made by all the parties concerned, accusations and threats of court action, as well as a lot of petty narrow-mindedness, including the then President's opinion on the building's shape, and the political opportunism, if not downright corruption, of those who made the decisions on the building. This dispute pitted politicians and librarians against each other (as well as the entire Czech cultural public), librarians against lawyers, lawyers against other lawyers, architects against other architects, the

---

44   "Klaus: Chobotnici na Letné zabráním i vlastním tělem," *iDNES* (3. 5. 2007); online: https://www.idnes.cz/zpravy/domaci/klaus-chobotnici-na-letne-zabranim-i -vlastnim telem.A070503_160531_domaci_pei [accessed 2020-04-03].

Design for a new National Library building (Jan Kaplický's architectural visualisation)

younger generation against the older and the then President against the former President (Václav Havel). Hundreds of articles, interviews and statements came out. There was even a television duel between then mayor Bém and architect Jan Kaplický.

In a nutshell, the entire case can be said to reflect Czech small-mindedness and inability to achieve consensus, as well as a crisis in values and criteria. The opportunistic political strategem, well-armed with legal arguments, had gained the upper hand over culture and the public interest. This was succinctly summed up by former President Václav Havel: "It is strange and perhaps symptomatic that the Czech public [...] are silent over monuments to banality such as the new building on Charles Square or the building on the corner of Wenceslas Square and 28th October Street opposite Koruna Palace [...] but when once every ten years someone designs something interesting, an original building, then the entire village is up in arms."[45]

---

45 Stanislav Dvořák, "Boj o chobotnici na Letné," *Novinky* (26. 10. 2007); online: https://www.novinky.cz/specialy/clanek/tema-boj-o-chobotnici-na-letne-39630 [accessed 2020-04-03].

... and all that's left (bus stop in Brno-Lesná)

This is a victory for Czech parochial conservativism and political demagoguery over modern-day architectural opinion and the needs of Czech reading culture.

COMPULSORY READING, *FAKE NEWS*

No other topic has attained such heights of media attention. Some attention has been aroused, albeit only over the short term, by the publication of the results of individual statistical surveys (of the adult and youth population), but because no earth-shattering findings are made in them, they are not such media dynamite, using empirical data instead to correct views that have generally been passed down that reading is on the wane, that people have stopped reading, that youngsters have turned away from reading completely and so forth.

Some attention was also aroused by the debate over "compulsory" school reading – i.e. what to recommend for children, what is appropriate for them and what is not; and where the time limits lie for when they are able to discern particulars. This discussion focused on *Babička* (Granny) by Božena Němcová, an iconic Czech reading book that was first published in 1855. The discussion included views expressed by several teachers reflecting their practical experience, with one of them saying: "Reading skill standards today are very low. Children are not able to absorb this complex text, and they get lost in it."[46] Another holds the view that it would be better to start with *Harry Potter* than with *Babička*. "The opportunities that open up are completely different when youngsters start telling you enthusiastically just how enthralled they were. That way they naturally get into literary interpretation – analysing the characters' psychology as the author intended it or how they would write it differently. That way the children enjoy Czech much more."[47] Young book influencer Lucie Zelinková expressed herself similarly: "Cramming *Babička* down primary schoolkids' throats is a fatal mistake, because at that age they can't understand it at all. They won't know why the teacher is forcing it on them and they'll never come back to it."[48]

In an online *iDNES* poll held in 2015 on whether *Babička* is appropriate compulsory reading material for children at primary school, 2,281 voted against and only 381 in favour, i.e. a ratio of six to one. These discussions centre around the general suitability of reading matter that is normatively recommended to children and around how to gain and hold their interest in reading. Hence in the Czech environment *Babička* came to be the *casus* of a small cultural war, albeit not as hard-fought as the new National Library building. The normative

---

46 "Babička po 150 letech děti už nezajímá," *iDNES* (29. 12. 2004); online: https://www.idnes.cz/kultura/literatura/babicka-po-150-letech-deti-uz-nezajima .A041229_113156_literatura_gra [accessed 2020-04-03]; see also Barbora Cihelková, "Zrušte Babičku, nerozumíme jí," *Lidové noviny* 13. 10. 2015, p. 14.
47 "Nahradí Babičku Harry Potter?", *iDNES* (17. 7. 2015); online: https://www .idnes.cz/zpravy/domaci/povinna-cetba-ve-skole.A150715_205812_domaci_zt [accessed 2020-04-03].
48 Anna Musilová, "Knižní influencerka: Češi jsou čtenáři. Cpát dětem Babičku je fatální chyba" (23. 8. 2017); online: https://www.idnes.cz/zpravy/lide-ceska /lucie-zelinkova-knizni-influencerka-rozhovor-lide-ceska.A170814_144631_lide -ceska_amu [accessed 2020-04-03].

The most iconic illustration from the most iconic Czech book - by Adolf Kašpar

defenders of the canon as something that is culturally binding on everyone are pitted against those who are instead trying to motivate pupils through pleasure in reading. This is also something of an internal pedagogical war between the younger and the older generations, i.e. between pedagogical traditionalists and liberals.

Another area where reading has risen to the fore, particularly in recent times, is the fight against *fake news*. The keywords that appear in this context are reading literacy, critical reading, information and disinformation, competence, danger, abuse, manipulation and propaganda. The Czech debate has much in common with debates taking place elsewhere, particularly in the West, the only possible specific feature being the great generational divide: the young, who are more informationally literate, have to look after the older ones who never attained such information literacy and who are thus more vulnerable to manipulation.

The Czech Republic saw a peak in digital manipulation during the last two presidential elections (2013 and 2018), which led many experts and socially engaged people to attempt some counter-activity. The other jeopardized group is schoolchildren. Several courses have been developed for teachers (e.g. Reading and writing for critical thinking), in an attempt to provide training and increase awareness and to ground reading literacy within the context of information, digital and media literacy. Literally an entire publication industry has arisen over fake news of various standards and levels of reliability. A prestige PR prize (*Novinářská křepelka* /Journalism Quail/) was awarded to Jakub Zelenka from Aktuálně.cz, who deals systematically with fake news and the war on disinformation.

There are numerous factors within this area that are emphasized – for example, the high toxicity of the material in question, the dangers and the caution required for working with information. However, most important of all is the struggle against the division of society, i.e. against its disintegration into segments that are going to carry on a cold war against each other, which will place society much more at the mercy of politicians, particularly the popularist kind.

READING COMMUNITIES

Here on the Czech scene too, a large proportion of reading life (i.e. actual practice) has shifted into the digital environment. It is repeatedly stated that literary criticism is losing its role, i.e. that it is ceasing to be a direction-indicator telling readers what to read. This goes hand in hand with its disappearance from the printed media. It is only being maintained systematically in literary magazines (e.g. *A2*, *Host and Tvar*) and a few of the social-cultural kind (e.g. *Respekt*).

This role has been taken over by various reading communities, bloggers, YouTubers and book influencers. It is within this environment that the primary reflection of what is being read among the readership can be seen. One influential platform is databazeknih.cz, more or less the Czech equivalent of Goodreads, presenting long-term ranking lists and annotated book titles with readers' discussion forums, news sections, lists of awards and publishers, as well as an Exchange and Mart section. This is truly a very busy platform with broad social scope. For many users it also functions as a bibliographical database, with both annotated titles and readers' subjective opinions. The platform has also taken over many of the roles of literary criticism. For example, the most popular book of 2017 was *Hana* by Alena Mornštajnová with 8,097 ratings and 2,489 comments.[49] On the long-term chart it came in second behind *Harry Potter and the Prisoner of Azkaban* by J. K. Rowling.

One advantage of this platform is its broad range, which really provides a good overview of what is being read and what is being thought about it, with all the social pathologies that such open public discussions bring up. One potential danger can be seen on Amazon, for example, not only in the advertisement and intrusion of other titles, but also in the doubts cast on the validity of some opinions. Is publishers' marketing not behind some of these views? And do not some of the negative opinions come from the competition?

The natural habitat for such shared, debated reading is increasingly coming to be Facebook, with its numerous communities focusing upon books, genres and reading, public and private, moderated strictly, laxly or not at all. Let us focus on just one of them, the one with the broadest scope. It is called *Co čteme* (What we are reading), it has 43,024 members[50] and it is private. Almost anything at all to do with reading is dealt with here: book tips (both requested and supplied), recommended literature for family members (mostly from parents to children), links to thought-provoking articles about books elsewhere, tips on reading methods, occasional polls, jokes about reading and books, furniture for reading (bookcases and armchairs), printed books versus e-books and so forth.

---

49 State as of 10 June 2020.
50 State as of 10 June 2020.

Let us present a couple of specific examples to provide a more three-dimensional perspective. "I need to recommend a book about the Holocaust for my thirteen-year-old daughter"; "Please can you recommend some humorous books." (interest in this kind of literature is very common); "Greetings to Stephen King fans and a question for them. Did they understand the ending of *The Long Walk* and as they read did they figure out just why it was all happening?"; "Over the last two weeks I've been unable to remember the name of the author of this short story: in 1889 a sickly child is born to an Austrian family. Some of his siblings have already died and if I remember well the author builds up the story in such a way that you keep your fingers crossed for the child and the entire family to survive. He gains your sympathy and it is only at the very end of the text that you find out this is Adolf Hitler"; "Is the place where you read a book important? Is it a good idea to eat while you read?" "Why do men enjoy reading on the toilet so much?" "Has anybody read anything by Noam Chomsky? I'm quite tempted. Thanks"; "I need a psychiatrist. I've just had my fifth unplanned trip past a bookshop this year." (the attached bill is for 744.60 CZK /29.1 EUR/).

The great virtue of a community like *Co čteme* is its vitality and thus the variety of its subjects and communication positions (information, adult education, warnings and so forth). At the same time it is very good "research material" for anyone dealing with the image of present-day reading. One disadvantage is the large number of contributions, which at a certain point can often overwhelm the discussions, rendering them opaque.

Thanks to a thesis by Martin Brzobohatý,[51] who investigated Czech reading group members' behaviour (i.e. not only those in *Co čteme*), we know that over one half (52%) of them look at postings at least once a day, while almost two fifths (38%) look at them at least once a week. We also know that almost three fifths (56%) of members do

---

51   Martin Brzobohatý, *Čtenářství a Facebook* (Brno: FF MU, 2017); online: https://is.muni.cz/th/spdkw/VerzeTisk.pdf [accessed 2020-04-03].

not contribute at all themselves and at the other extreme 0.5% of members contribute every day. As for those who comment on postings, these are most commonly represented by those who comment less than once a month (36%), followed by those who do not comment at all (32%). Over one half (55%) of members of these groups belong to the aforementioned databazeknih.cz.

WRITERS AND READERS

Writers' complaints that they are not being read or that other books are being read rather than those which ought to be are among the long-term *loci communes* of culture in general. Something of a silent but constant cultural war is being played out. Moreover, the Czech scene is distinctive in that ever since the National Revival in the 19th century writers have received considerable social recognition. This is associated with the role played by language and the key role it has played in the formation of national culture. Ever since then, writers have been tagged with the memorable description of "clairvoyants" and "prophets". Even under Communism, writers enjoyed considerable appreciation, albeit only those who were willing to provide support – see Stalin's famous description of writers as the "engineers of human souls". In other words, reading "prophets" is either a sacred patriotic task or it is supposed to be contingent upon the cultural-technological project of "engineers of human souls".

It was not until the post-1989 period that relations between writers and readers were completely settled. This was a time when an unprecedented amount of books came out, which inevitably diluted attention. Shelf life in bookshops was shortened, thus shortening the time for new titles to bask in the light of public attention. Many writers, particularly those belonging to the older and middle generations, have not taken kindly to this turnaround, as they are not used to dealing with readers, let alone soliciting them, because the main issue in their lives had been their struggles to get their books published at all. In other words, they had been fighting the censors and administrative obstacles, not fighting for readers. These were times of great hunger among readers, when there was great interest in almost anything in print that was at least to some extent attractive or alluring. And now this hunger among readers has turned into satiety.

How do Czech writers react to this? One position is to defend their own writing as an entirely autonomous activity, i.e. the kind that must not take any account of the reader – i.e. the familiar "I don't think of the readers when I write – I write mainly for myself" routine, which we would primarily expect to come from older authors, but that is not the case. It also frequently occurs among the young, i.e. those who have already learnt to swim in the cold waters of the book glut. For example, this is how young prose writer Jana Šrámková described herself: "I pay no heed to the readers. Whether I am writing for adults or for children, my texts are mainly for myself so that I can enjoy them just like my readers." [52] One alternative to this position might be the declaration made by Antonín Bajaja, who is more of an older generation writer: "I think that Czech literature is lacking more better-quality readers."[53] The former example was more a defence of extreme authorial autonomy, while the latter is a schoolmasterly sigh.

We find a greater perceptivity towards the opposite end of the communication field among writers with mainstream tastes, but this only widens the gulf in public awareness. For those who see themselves as "highbrow" literature writers, these testimonies only confirm that they should not at all concern themselves with any such thing as readers. Numbers of copies sold are thus for them frequently an argument against the quality of the work, and evidence of its superficial and simplistic nature. In one rather unrestrained discussion over Alena Mornštajnová, the most frequently read Czech author of the last few years, another young Czech author, Ivana Myšková,

---

52   Jana Šrámková, "Na cestách s paní Dallowayovou ," interview with Ondřej Kavalír, *Grand Biblio* 3 (2009), no. 11, p. 5.
53   Antonín Bajaja, "Chybí mi tu dobří čtenáři", interview with Ondřej Nezbeda, *Respekt* 21 (2010), no. 12, p. 41.

Alena Mornštajnová, one of the most popular Czech authors today

says quite unequivocally: "But for me to be able to say anything decent about her writing I would have to have read her books, which I haven't. And I don't really want to either, because I know that what entertains others is not going to entertain me."[54] Hence the fact that a lot of people read it is clear proof of a lack of literary quality. Fortunately, this discussion also included the very reasonable and conciliatory voice of another author and publisher, Markéta Hejkalová: "It seems to me to be uncollegial and actually quite senseless to condemn books you have not read just because lots of other people read

---

54 https://www.facebook.com/tereza.semotamova [accessed 2020-04-03].

them. Myself, I admire the art of writing a substantial story that gets to be a bestseller. That is a great service to literature."[55]

The field of communication still appears to be polarized in Manichaean fashion, particularly with regard to the writers, and especially those who rank themselves in the "highbrow" literature category, as if the National Revival model of the writer as a prophet had been revived amongst them: in one corner high literary demands and in the other the reader. The reflection of literature as principally a communication entity, i.e. the awareness that it always takes two, is not all that evident among Czech writers. The way writers in the First Republic managed to move beyond their artistic programmes, reflect phenomena on their margins (e.g. Karel Čapek) and deal with the needs of the reader (and not just of the "elite"), has also been lost from cultural memory.

SUMMARY AND CONCLUSIONS

One subject that made a powerful impact on public debate was the construction of the National Library. Attention was drawn by all the controversies that it faced, many of which stemmed from its untraditional form. The subject was also highly politicized, with its primary polarization axis being the cultural public on the one hand and the politicians and lawyers on the other. Remarkably, funding for the construction was not the central issue here, as it could have been raised successfully in many ways. The debate and its conclusion were also affected by the death of architect Jan Kaplický in 2009.

These debates also indicate just how substantially the relationship had changed between the writer and reader. The latter was now the predominant force in the literary field, who needed to be solicited and not just taken for granted as the precondition for literary communication, while many authors did not know how to deal with this new situation. Some of them were hampered by their generational

---

55   Ibid.

luggage – they simply weren't accustomed to anything like this. Others understood their privileged involvement in "highbrow" literature to be so assured that they did not consider it necessary, appropriate or desirable to deal with this issue at all. However, there are also authors who – thanks to the social networks in particular – have managed to take control of the field and thus substantially increase their social capital.

5
From the statistical standpoint

Although a start was made in the chapter on the present-day situation, in this chapter the statistics will now provide us with the full background. We will chiefly focus on the main data on reading. We base ourselves on four representative polls of the Czech population: 15+ from 2007, 2010, 2013 and 2018 and then two polls of the youth population (2013/2014 and 2017),[56] homing in on the multiple aspects of reading – how much we read, how often we read, what we read and why we read. Reading in the digital environment will also find its place.

BASIC DATA

Let us begin with an executive summary of the main statistical indices involved in Czech reading culture.

Based on four representative statistical polls of readers and reading in the Czech Republic (dating from 2007, 2010, 2013 and 2018), organized by the Czech National Library and the Institute of Czech Literature at the Czech Academy of Sciences, Czech reading culture can be said to show:

– *a large number of readers,* i.e. of those who read at least one book a year (in 2018 these made up 78% of the population aged 15+); it is not a result that places the Czech population at the very summit of the European figures, where the Scandinavian countries and the Netherlands belong, but just beneath them;

---

56 For technical details see Appendix 1.

- a consistent *period of time* (around 30 minutes a day) spent reading books;
- a strong *disinclination towards reading magazines* (particularly among the youngest age cohorts – 15–24);
- a large *gender gap* – a big difference between women and men (in favour of women); while this gap can be found everywhere, it is rather larger in the Czech Republic;
- almost *no age gap;* reading only decreases in middle age, which is an inevitable result of the life cycle and can also be found elsewhere; the age gap only appears online for digital reading (in favour of the youngest);
- a very *small urbanization gap:* the size of the town or city plays practically no role at all;
- much expanded *domestic libraries:* in 2018 only 2% of the population stated they had no books at home; the average number of books in a Czech household is 253;
- the attitude toward*s public libraries* is still quite positive, even though the number of visitors to them is gradually declining (in 2007 it was 41%, in 2018 it was 28%);
- the propensity to see books as *gifts* has grown much stronger;
- books are still mostly acquired in a conservative manner (in bricks-and-mortar bookshops), even though the proportion bought online is increasing;
- there is a strong feeling on the book market that there is a *glut of books:* in 2013, there were seven times as many of those who said they did not buy books because there were too many on the market as those who said there were not enough;
- the trend towards *e-books* is not all that strong (particularly in comparison with the USA and UK);
- there is a preference primarily for contemporary entertaining literature (detective stories, thrillers, romances and so forth): the most popular author in recent research has been the Norwegian novelist Jo Nesbø and the most popular book was *Harry Potter* (both the entire series and its individual parts) by J. K. Rowling.

In this survey of the three mainstays of reading culture (reading [books], book buying and visiting public libraries) the picture looks like this:

Graph 5.1   Three key parameters of Czech reading culture (2007, 2010, 2013, 2018)

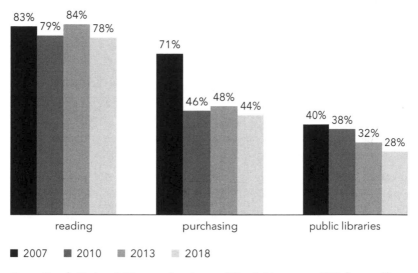

reading   purchasing   public libraries

■ 2007   ■ 2010   ■ 2013   ▫ 2018

Source Czech National Library – Institute of Czech Literature, CAS (base: all)

A brief explanation: anyone who has stated that over the last year they have read at least one book of any kind (fiction, non-fiction or educational) and for any purpose (entertainment, information or study) is deemed to be a reader. A buyer is deemed to be anybody who has stated that over the past year they have bought at least one book (for themselves or for somebody else), while the public library column is filled in by anybody who has stated that over the past year they have visited a public library at least once (and not just to borrow books).

What do we find? We find that the first column (*reading*) is maintaining relative momentum. Whether or not the falling trend shown by the figures from the last survey will carry on remains to be seen.

The value of the median (the figure that divides the population into two equal halves) is the same for the last two surveys – five books. For *Book market* we see a big change between the first and second surveys, which was caused by three factors: (1) a slightly altered methodology; (2) the economic crisis of 2008–2009, which did have an effect on our shopping – specifically, that it threw items not included in our basic living needs (i.e. books) out of our "market basket"; (3) the book glut, or surplus, begins to make itself felt, i.e. the fact that books act as big competition for each other. In *Public libraries* we see a gradual decline in the numbers of those who go to them, although this decline is compensated for by visits online, as other statistics show us. Public libraries have mainly lost their clientele because during this period they have ceased to be locations providing public internet access, which was still an important service provided at the beginning of the 21st century, particularly in small Czech towns. The internet also deprived them of many visitors – particularly due to the permanent accessibility of basic reference works (*Wikipedia*, language dictionaries and the like). For example, in the past if secondary school pupils had to write essays for homework and did not have the appropriate literature in their bookcase, their only other option was to visit a public library.

Graph 5.2   Reading books – four parameters (2018)

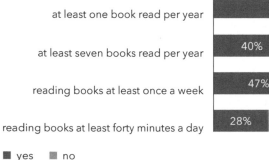

Source Czech National Library – Institute of Czech Literature, CAS (base: all)

We may define the statistical reader under various criteria. Although this is a rather arbitrary issue, it should always be resolved logically. The following graph presents a couple of these options based on data from the last survey (2018).

In the case of readers it is necessary to follow both the numbers of books read (the first two lines) and the time spent on reading them, which we can follow either as a frequency (third line) or as a rate (fourth column).

The first line (One book read per year) defines the reader on the basis of a criterion that is used in other surveys (Germany, USA, Poland, EU), a criterion involving a certain cultural minimalism – something like a fulfilled obligation towards reading culture. This criterion is met by over three quarters of the Czech adult population. The second criterion (seven books read per year) involves those for whom reading is a more regular activity, albeit not yet entirely regular. This criterion is matched by two fifths of the Czech population. The third line (reading books at least once a week) shows that reading is also an activity that requires a certain regularity, for which a week is neither too little nor too much. This criterion is matched by almost half of the population. The final line sets the strictest conditions for readers, laying down a time limit on reading during an average day. This condition is met by a little more than one quarter of the Czech adult population.

We shall now look in more detail at the market satiety phenomenon, examined in the following table, which attempts to indicate something like a *book hunger index*.

Table 5.1   Reading, purchasing and public libraries (2007–2010–2013–2018)

	2007	2010	2013	2018
ratio of buyers to readers	0.9	0.6	0.6	0.6
ratio of visitors (to public libraries) to readers	0.5	0.5	0.4	0.4
total	1.4	1.1	1.0	1.0

Source: Czech National Library – Institute of Czech Literature, CAS (base: all)

This table requires a brief explanation. The level of the entire reading culture is expressed primarily as a percentage of those who read, i.e. where a lot of reading is being done, one can expect a greater interest in the book market and in public libraries. In other words, the number of readers increases the volume of the entire reading culture and expands the reading public. Other activities are then derived from this index. Very clearly, this index refers to the acquisition of books. The book hunger index indicates the book satiety of our reading culture, or rather the satiation of the need for them. The higher this index, the greater the need, while the lower this index, the lower the need. Index 0 would mean we are reading without needing to acquire books through the two main channels, clearly drawing on some other channels (most probably from domestic libraries). Index 2 would mean that our acquisition of books is entirely dependent upon the two main channels. Theoretically, the book hunger index could be higher than 2, which would mean that we are acquiring books at a far greater rate than we are reading them.

Why a book hunger index and not an index of some other reading material? The question arises here whether or not to adhere to the book as a standard when numerous investigations[57] have shown us that reading is continually expanding into other areas, as was evident even before the digital revolution, which has only highlighted this trend.

Because the book continues to appear to be the most fundamental code of our culture, and not just of our reading culture. Ever since the invention of writing we have been living in the "order of books" (cf. Roger Chartier).[58] The book has entered our imagery and

---

57   E.g. Roger E. Bohn – James E. Short, *How Much Information? Report on American Consumers* (San Diego: Global Information Industry Center – University of California, 2009); online: https://group47.com/HMI_2009_ConsumerReport _Dec9_2009.pdf [accessed 2020-04-05]; Adriaan van der Weel, *Changing Our Textual Minds. Towards a Digital Order of Knowledge* (Manchester – New York: Manchester University Press, 2011).
58   Roger Chartier, *The Order of Books*, transl. by Lydia G. Cochrane (Stanford: Stanford University Press, 1994 [1992]); See also Adriaan van der Weel. *Changing Our Textual Minds*, p. 3.

overflowed far beyond the boundaries of the printed world.[59] Thus we read "in the book of life" or "in the book of nature" and we say of somebody educated that he or she speaks "like a book"; when we agree on something and consider it to be binding then we say you can "enter it in the books". The book is a unit of completion, completeness, closedness and orderliness, both from the author's and the reader's standpoint. It is a symbol of knowledge and memory. Moreover, the data both here and elsewhere indicate that anyone who reads books reads everything else as well to a large extent. There is also a quite long tradition of other surveys. The criterion of a read book is not even abandoned in the digital age, since all the other kinds (particularly digital reading) are simply added to it. Even these days "book reading is indeed the best predictor of reading skill among children who have grown up with digital devices, the so-called digital natives" (Hildegunn Støle).[60]

READERS AND NON-READERS

Let us now turn to those who are the main bearers of reading culture, indeed its very purpose – the readers. The following graph shows a breakdown of readers based on the number of books they read per year.

This graph portrays a shift that was not too radical but still very evident; frequent readers, i.e. those who read more than average. are gradually declining in number, while the rest do not show any discernible trend.

---

59   See e.g.. Małgorzata Skibińska, "Książka. Symbolika, metaforyka." In Anna Żbikowska-Migoń – Marta Skalska-Zlat (eds.), *Encyklopedia książki* (Wrocław: Wydawnictwo Uniwersytetu Wrocławskiego, 2017), pp. 216-221.
60   Hildegunn Støle, "Why digital natives need books: The myth of the digital native," *First Monday* 23 (2018), no. 10, non-paged; online: https://journals.uic .edu/ojs/index.php/fm/article/view/9422/7594 [accessed 2019-04-15].

Graph 5.3   Reader breakdown (2007, 2010, 2013, 2018)[61]

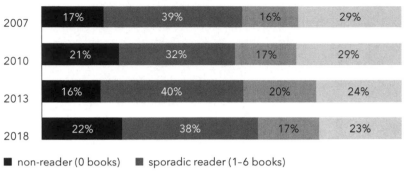

2007	17%	39%	16%	29%
2010	21%	32%	17%	29%
2013	16%	40%	20%	24%
2018	22%	38%	17%	23%

■ non-reader (0 books)   ■ sporadic reader (1–6 books)
■ regular reader (7–12 books)   ▨ frequent reader (13+ books)

Source: Czech National Library – Institute of Czech Literature, CAS (base: all)

It might be objected that this is merely an "ivory tower distinction", i.e. that numbers and automatic delimitations do not yet reveal any fundamental positions, but this is not entirely the case. The actual frequency of reading, expressed here as the number of books read, is also linked to the quality of reading, as well as the extent of its cultural anchorage. For example, a PISA tests tell us that there is a correlation between the quality of the results and the frequency of reading.

The non-reader (0 books) – we see it works out that anybody who does not even read a single book finds himself or herself beyond reading culture, i.e. without any need to participate in it. Now strictly speaking, no one can end up outside reading culture, because they are already a part of a society that has been fully literate for a hundred years, but they are its "stowaways". They say that they have no time or that they do not enjoy reading, i.e. that they make do with other media. Numerous correlations in other activities show the non-reader to be someone quite different from others. There is a far

---

61   Where the total does not come to 100%, this is because figures have been rounded up or down to whole percentages.

stronger dividing line between them and the others than between other parts of the spectrum (i.e. the three other types of readers).

The sporadic reader (1-6 books) – his or her activity is to a large extent sporadic. This is most likely someone who just intermittently reaches for a book, for example on holiday. Reading is just a marginal supplement to their other activities, whether cultural or not. These are often people who will refer to a book on the express recommendation of someone around them, whom they have allowed to talk them into it, or they may only reach for a book when they have no other activity to hand and they have enough time on their hands. They primarily read pragmatically (*I have to*) – reference books, textbooks and so forth.

The regular reader (7–12 books) – books are their constant companions, particularly during their leisure time, but not even here is any planned, systematic reading involved. They read because they are used to reading. They are generally surrounded by other people who also read, so they have a quite extensive social infrastructure that has been created around them that bears them aloft. To a large extent they are able to disengage from pragmatic reading (*I have to*) in favour of reading out of interest and for the experience (*I want to*).

The frequent reader (13+ books) – this really does involve systematic reading, often with more than one book being read at the same time. Here the reader is also interested to a far greater extent than the others are in information about books and other reading materials. This is a truly committed kind of reader, i.e. one for whom reading is the main activity, both cultural and otherwise. These are passionate readers (fifty plus books read a year) – who make up some 5.5% – 6.5% of the Czech population.

It will not be without benefit to look at the socio-demographic profiles concerned. Let us consider the two extremes:
– *the non-reader*: most likely a man, who has not passed the school-leaving exam, working physically, probably from the lowest income category; in terms of professions these are most frequently

represented by manual workers, shop assistants, drivers and the like.

- *the frequent reader:* most likely a woman, aged either 15–24 or 65+, educated up to school-leaving exam standard at least, probably in the higher income categories but economically inactive, out of all professions this category is dominated by pensioners.

Let us now focus on readers and non-readers (of books) in terms of the reasons they give. For the former, why they read, and for the latter, why they do not read.

Readers. Their motivation for reading (books) – simplified into two main categories –, is divided into two roughly equal halves: 48% say they read for information and knowledge, 52% for entertainment and the emotional experience.

Non-readers. Slightly over one third (34%) say they have no time, while almost one third (28%) say they do not enjoy reading; over one fifth (22%) say they do not need to read for anything, because they obtain everything they need from other media; roughly one is six (16%) say they used to read books, but not any more. We should only consider the second and subsequent items relevant, because the "no time" response is just a very convenient option which basically serves as an escape route that does not compel respondents to seek deeper reasons.

Among *fiction readers,* the gender gap has been growing far more in favour of women. The probability that a book reader (in general) is going to be a reader of fiction books is 86%; i.e. approximately just one (book) reader in six is purely and exclusively a reader of non-fiction books, hence there is extensive overlap here, no matter how varied the reasons why people read fiction are – most frequently for relaxation followed by enrichment of internal life and in third place as a source of information. Readers most frequently choose fiction based on genre (23%), author (18%) and recommendations from acquaintances and those closer to them (17.5%).

Only 1% state that they read *poetry* regularly, 27% read it at least occasionally or have read it at one time in the past. This means that even those who must inevitably have come across poetry during their schooldays and so had an obligation to at least read some, do not actually own up to this.

As regards *reading magazines*, those for women enjoy the greatest popularity among Czech readers, followed by the social-political kind and special-interest (hobbies), lifestyle, sports and specialist magazines. Out of all the individual types of magazines there is a large gender and age polarization. Predominant among women are lifestyle and women's magazines, while men read significantly more of the sporting and hobby-oriented or special-interest kind. The youngest (15-24) prefer youth magazines, while the oldest (65+) prefer women's and religious magazines. Those with the highest education prefer social-political and specialist magazines considerably more than anybody else.

READING IN THE DIGITAL SPHERE

In line with expectations, the key differentiating sign among digital users (internauts) is age: in the 15–24 cohort we find 95% of those who use the internet every day (total abstainers, i.e. those who do not use the internet at all, come to just 1%), while in the 65+ cohort they come to 27% (with complete abstainers coming to 51%). An important role is also played, albeit to a lesser extent, by education – as the more educated we are, the more we use it – among those without the school-leaving examination certificate we find 22% of total internet abstainers, while this figure is just 5% amongst graduates.

The socio-demographic profile of an internaut, i.e. an internet user, is as follows:

– somewhat more likely to be a man (though the gender gap is not large), from the 15–24 age cohort, probably educated to graduate level, probably from a higher income bracket, probably economically active, probably from professions requiring mental work.

Internauts have had a wide selection to choose from, but only texts of a public nature (not emails, Facebook statuses and so forth).[62] The predominance of pragmatic-service genres is evident.

Graph 5.4   What we are reading online (2018)

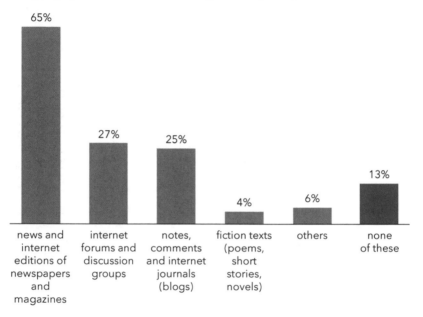

Source: Czech National Library – Institute of Czech Literature, CAS (base: internet users)

If we counted up this data to 100%, it would work out that almost one half (47%) belongs to the first category.

The following graph indicates which of these we prefer when reading e-books.[63]

---

62   Several answers possible, total ≠ 100 %.
63   Several answers possible, total ≠ 100 %.

Graph 5.5 Which devices we use to read e-books (2018)

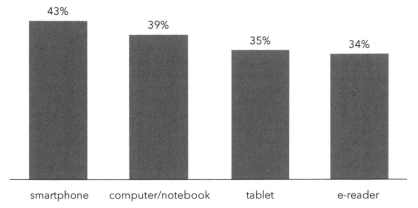

| smartphone | computer/notebook | tablet | e-reader |

Source: Czech National Library – Institute of Czech Literature, CAS (base: internet users)

Perhaps surprisingly the e-reader comes in last, even though we are asking specifically about e-books. However, this trend has recently (since about 2012) been evident all over the world, as its rise, starting in 2007 with the first version of Amazon's Kindle, has come to a halt.

Talking of the digital sphere, it only remains for us to look at how often we open books; here we present both printed books and audio-books for comparison.

What do we find? That just less than one fifth of the adult population (19%) use e-books, and even fewer use audio-books (19%). The number of regular readers of printed books is eight times higher than the number of readers of e-books and 33 times higher than the number of audio-book listeners.

Graph 5.6   Printed books, e-books and audio-books – how often (2018)

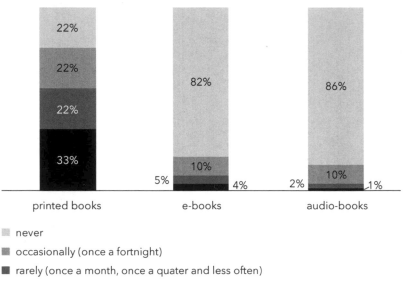

never

occasionally (once a fortnight)

rarely (once a month, once a quater and less often)

regularly (daily/several times a week)

Source: Czech National Library – Institute of Czech Literature, CAS (base: all)

READING AND OTHER MEDIA ACTIVITIES

It is now about a century since reading lost its monopoly over information. Since around that time we have been living in media polygamy, and it has come to be just one of several media activities. Let us now imagine this "media pie-graph" of the number of minutes we spend on individual media during an average day, though it does have to be pointed out at the same time that it is becoming increasingly difficult to say where one medium begins and another one ends. The boundaries are getting blurred, particularly with regard to user behaviour. We watch television on the internet (live or from the archive), we listen to the radio, stream music and download movies from Netflix and YouTube. On the social networks we read articles

Graph 5.7 Media activities (2007, 2010, 2013, 2018) – minutes/day[64]

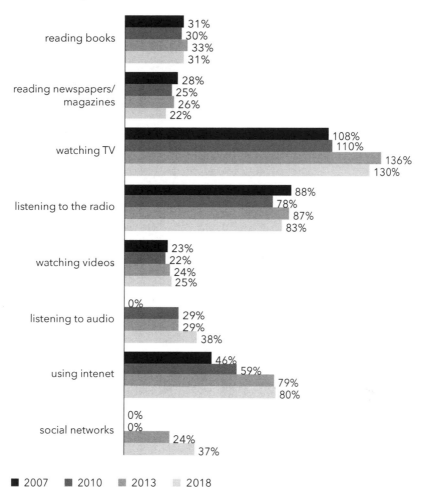

reading books
31%
30%
33%
31%

reading newspapers/ magazines
28%
25%
26%
22%

watching TV
108%
110%
136%
130%

listening to the radio
88%
78%
87%
83%

watching videos
23%
22%
24%
25%

listening to audio
0%
29%
29%
38%

using intenet
46%
59%
79%
80%

social networks
0%
0%
24%
37%

■ 2007　■ 2010　■ 2013　　2018

Source: Czech National Library – Institute of Czech Literature, CAS (base: all)

---

64   Watching videos (e.g. DVDs, YouTube, Stream etc.), listening to music (e.g. from a tape recorder, CD/DVDs, mp3s, the internet etc.); reading books and reading newspapers/magazines – in both cases in printed and electronic forms.

that someone in our community has posted to us. We often behave very intuitively online, i.e. without actually knowing where we find ourselves at any given moment. I might be reading an article from an online version of a newspaper (i.e. a news item), or am I already in the part that runs under the online section (i.e. the part that is just on the internet)? Let us move on with all these "buts" to the following table. A very popular format among the young in particular is podcasts, which offer a relatively new way to disseminate information (having only been invented in 2004) that can be downloaded and listened to for free, while it is the listener who chooses what to listen to, thus differentiating it from radio.

Book reading shows a constant value of around thirty minutes per day, whereas for magazine reading we can observe a decline over time, which to a large extent is clearly the result of what we have described above – many readers have moved this activity to the internet (or to digital sphere), so these minutes are allocated there. The increase for television in 2013 has a specific domestic explanation. That was the time the entire Czech Republic converted from analog broadcasting to cable, which resulted in a significant increase in channels. This also goes to explain the increased interest shown in the greater number of daily TV minutes. The growth of the internet and social networks is evident and understandable.

It will be of benefit to combine this information with another graph showing the numbers of those who do not spend a single minute on particular media activities.

This way we arrive at something like an *inclusivity index*, i.e. information on the extent to which individual media activities are combined with our everyday activities. A developmental view (2007–2018) shows that in the case of book reading, the quarter of non-users grew into one third, and in the case of magazines the number of daily non-readers increased almost fourfold; as for watching TV, the number of non-users doubled, and in the case of radio, there was a constant large rise in the number of non-users, which has almost doubled since 2007. Watching videos is in a more or less stable state. Listening

Graph 5.8 Non-users – o minutes per day (2007, 2010, 2013, 2018)[65]

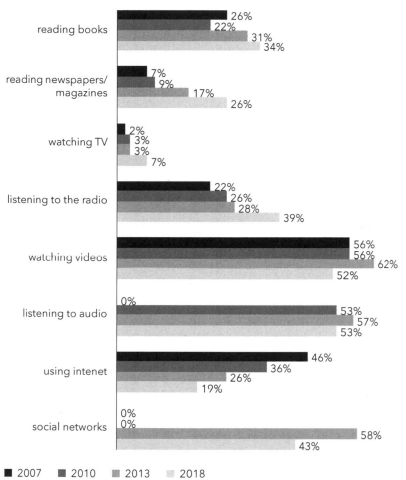

Source: Czech National Library – Institute of Czech Literature, CAS (base: all)

---

65 "0%" means that in the year in question there was no survey of media activity.

to audio is also in a more or less stable state. The internet has shown a marked decrease in non-users, with almost every second person a non-user in 2007 turning into almost every sixth in 2018. As for social networks the decline has been from three fifths to two fifths.

Hence the most inclusive medium, i.e. the one that reaches the greatest number of users, is still television. The internet has risen to second place, while reading newspapers and magazines is now in third place. The least inclusive medium is audio.

We might also check out which media correlate positively with book reading, which negatively and which are neutral:
- positive relations: reading magazines, listening to the radio, using the internet, listening to music;
- negative relations: watching television, watching videos (all media);
- neutral relations: social networks.

The order of elements in a row indicates the extent of the correlation. We see that reading books is associated in a significantly positive way with other media (specifically, reading, audio and the internet, which is a medium of all kinds); a negative association is shown by visual media.

READERS' PREFERENCES

Apart from the number of books read and the time spent on reading, we should also be interested in what is actually being read, as this is precisely what reflects our preferences. The following table of data from 2018 presents information on the Czech population's approach to different kinds of reading. The responses were provided by those who declared themselves to be readers (who have read at least one book per year), where up to three answers were possible (see also Appendices 4–6).[66]

---

66 Total of items ≠ 100 %.

Graph 5.9 What we are reading (2018)

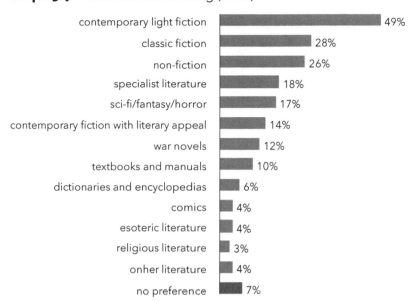

contemporary light fiction 49%
classic fiction 28%
non-fiction 26%
specialist literature 18%
sci-fi/fantasy/horror 17%
contemporary fiction with literary appeal 14%
war novels 12%
textbooks and manuals 10%
dictionaries and encyclopedias 6%
comics 4%
esoteric literature 4%
religious literature 3%
onher literature 4%
no preference 7%

Source: Czech National Library – Institute of Czech Literature, CAS (base: readers)

From the socio-demographic standpoint, some very strong polarizations predominate here (men/ women, younger/older and so forth). For the most frequently read kinds see the following graph. Men prefer non-fiction. The youngest prefer textbooks and reference works, along with sci-fi, fantasy and horror (here their predominance is truly enormous). At our most advanced age our leisure preference is not only contemporary fiction but also classic fiction – as our interest in it increases with age. Likewise our interest in non-fiction increases with age. Middle age (35–54) is a period when none of the reading types predominates. As the level of education rises so does interest in most types of reading, particularly classic fiction, non-fiction and specialist literature. The only kinds of literature where the opposite tendency predominates is sci-fi, fantasy and horror, as well as comics and to some extent war literature.

Graph 5.10 Contemporary leisure fiction (2018)

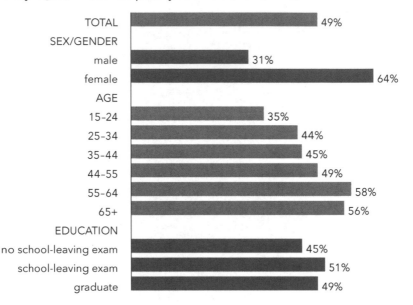

TOTAL — 49%
SEX/GENDER
male — 31%
female — 64%
AGE
15-24 — 35%
25-34 — 44%
35-44 — 45%
44-55 — 49%
55-64 — 58%
65+ — 56%
EDUCATION
no school-leaving exam — 45%
school-leaving exam — 51%
graduate — 49%

Source: Czech National Library – Institute of Czech Literature, CAS (base: readers)

Above all we see a conspicuous gender polarization (with twice as many women as men); an increase with age can also be observed; in contrast, education does not play a strong differentiating role at all and the same applies to the size of the town of residence.

This somewhat problematizes the traditional view that people with the highest education read this kind of literature less than people with lower educational achievements. It is generally the case that reading correlates with education, so the higher the level of the former, the stronger is the latter. This is an indisputable fact. However, this graph (and some of the other information) indicates that strong readership is primarily readership with a *broad range*, and only then *elite* readership, i.e. the more challenging types of books (contemporary fiction with literary appeal and non-fiction).

FAMILY AND SCHOOL

Now we come to readers' socialization. We arrive backwards at this statistical area from the current phase, going back in time – we enquire about the background, i.e. about what was experienced before. Hence we are not merely seeking the socio-demographic association, but also the socialization. To be specific, two important instances – developmentally the first and the second.

First let us focus on parents and their reader profiles.

Graph 5.11 Mothers and fathers as readers (2018)

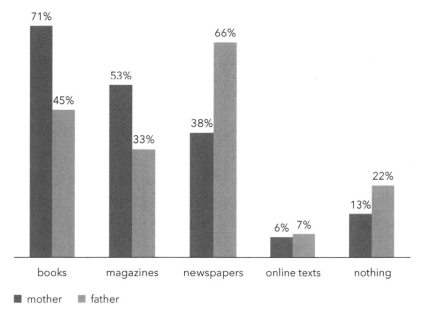

Source: Czech National Library – Institute of Czech Literature, CAS (base: all)

The predominance of mothers in the case of books is only to be expected, just like the predominance of fathers in the case of newspapers. The gender gap is also to be expected, even though here it is substantially wider than for the population as a whole. If we introduce something like a readership total (cultural capital),[67] then mothers have 168% and fathers 151%.

It will be useful to associate this category with our four kinds of readers by means of correlations.

Graph 5.12 Parents who have read nothing and categories of readers (2018)

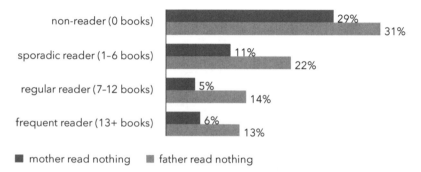

■ mother read nothing   ■ father read nothing

Source: Czech National Library – Institute of Czech Literature, CAS (Base: all)

We see that the negative cultural capital (non-reading parents) that a non-reader in the family receives is around three and a half times greater than that received by the frequent reader, and approximately twice as much as that received by the sporadic reader.

We believe that this is a very important finding. A cultural pessimist might say that in about two-thirds of families with reading parents, non-readers ultimately emerged, while a cultural optimist has the opportunity to point out: look, even from every tenth family where there was no reading at home a frequent reader can emerge, and at the same time it is clearly confirmed that parents' reading has a strong association with the kind of readers their children ultimately turn out to be. And there is also the cultural realist: the family

---

67   With no "nothing" item.

as a primary socialization medium need not provide some definitive predetermination for our subsequent reading career, but at the same time it is an indisputable fact that non-reading parents place a much greater burden on their children's subsequent lives than reading parents. In other words, something resembling a handicap race has been set up for non-reading parents' children's lives.

One important instance is that of reading out loud, particularly up to the age when we start to read for ourselves, i.e. at six years old. Its role does not only involve pre-reading training, as it also plays a considerable socialization role, i.e. the proximity and time provided by those closest to us are of importance.

Graph 5.13 Reading aloud when we were children (2018)

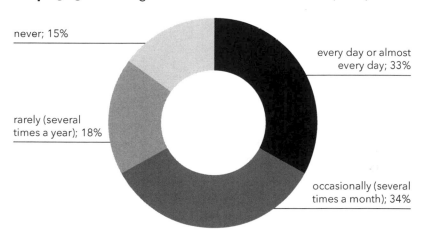

never; 15%

every day or almost
every day; 33%

rarely (several
times a year); 18%

occasionally (several
times a month); 34%

Source: Czech National Library – Institute of Czech Literature, CAS (base: all)

Over two-thirds (67%) of the population of the Czech Republic aged 15+ remember being read to at least occasionally. One third were read to either sporadically (18%) or not at all (15%). A substantial role is also played by age – as the older we get the less we read out or have read out loud, which is obviously to do with the fact that in the past reading aloud at home was not paid so much attention, particularly in rural families.

A home library is all part and parcel of domestic arrangements. The very physical presence of books plays a role in reader socialization. Moreover, home libraries are historically among the basic cultural and educational foundations of Czech culture (see also pp. 134–136), particularly in times when it was not possible due to prohibitions and censorship to rely on the public libraries' collections and the range offered by the book market.

Graph 5.14   Home libraries - number of items (2007, 2010, 2013, 2018)

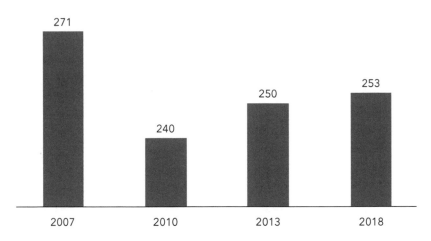

Source: Czech National Library – Institute of Czech Literature, CAS (base: all)

A more or less stable state predominates here. The only substantial change took place between the first and the second surveys.

The largest item is the total of 100–199 books (19%), the second is 50–99 books (17%), third place is taken by the 500+ item (14%). Only 5% of the population have more than one thousand books in their libraries.

The socio-demographic indices have not altered at all: larger libraries are owned by women and people with the highest education, as well as the most elderly. On the other hand we find the smallest libraries among the 25–34 age cohort, i.e. precisely at the age when most are establishing a family. Out of all the regions, Prague stands out very conspicuously (360 books; Bohemia 247; Moravia/Czech Silesia 223). It is also the case that the older our children at home, the larger our libraries are.

School emerges as the second environment, where reader socialization expands to include another instance – teachers and classmates. One of the teaching tools used is known as "compulsory" (though nowadays it is known as recommended) reading, i.e. titles that are considered mandatory to read (or at least to know).

Graph 5.15 Attitude to compulsory/recommended reading (2018)

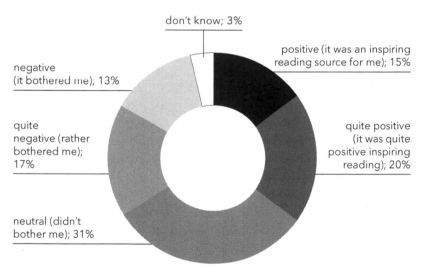

don't know; 3%

positive (it was an inspiring reading source for me); 15%

negative (it bothered me); 13%

quite positive (it was quite positive inspiring reading); 20%

quite negative (rather bothered me); 17%

neutral (didn't bother me); 31%

Source: Czech National Library – Institute of Czech Literature, CAS (base: all)

Here the range has been divided into three approximately equal sized parts: one third (35%) see it positively, one third (31%) neutrally and one third (30%) negatively. The 15–24 age cohort is the only one where the negative answers outweigh the positive. The most positive attitutude to compulsory reading can be seen among the most elderly (65+). The trend is clear: the older we get, the more positive our attitude towards compulsory reading becomes. Out of the other variables, an important role is also played by the kind of work involved, particularly in the case of mental work. As for the amount of income per head, the most positive attitudes towards compulsory reading belong to those from the highest income categories. However, both within the latter category are linked to education by their very nature.

CHILDREN

We also have reliable empirical data (from 2014 and 2017) on the reading culture of the young population (6–14). This data is collected in slightly different ways which take more account of the specific nature of this age group (for technical details see Appendix 2). The link to leisure time, connection with school performance and the parents' reading background is examined to a far greater extent.

For all indices readership is divided into junior (6– 9) and senior (10–14) school age. This is shown in the following graph.

As can be seen, positive attitude towards reading goes down with age. In the youngest age cohorts it is still two-thirds (64%), but amongst the oldest it comes to less than one half (46%)

The focus was also on images of readership, i.e. the ideas that children associate with reading, as well as the reasons why they turn to books. Foremost amongst these is "if a book grabs me", second and third "if I have to hand in some compulsory school reading" and "if I get a new book as a present". In contrast the most frequent reason why children do not read is that "I can't read very well yet. I'm no good at it," and then "reading is too much of an effort. There are

Graph 5.16   Do you enjoy reading books? Children aged 6-14, (2017)

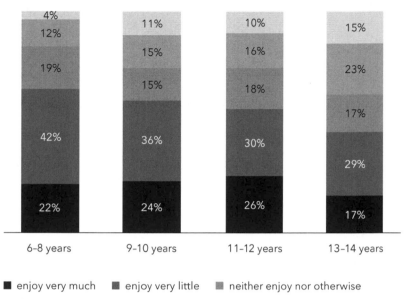

| | enjoy very much | | enjoy very little | | neither enjoy nor otherwise |
| | don't enjoy much | | don't enjoy at all |

Source: Czech National Library (base: all)

lots of more enjoyable things than reading books," or just "I don't enjoy it."

It has been shown that reading books correlates strongly with high grades at school, and not only in subjects that are linked in some way to reading (Czech language and foreign languages). The following graph shows a correlation between grades and the number of books read (over the last school year).

What other substantial findings have emerged from research into the young population?

– that a directive approach to setting "compulsory" school reading (without any personal initiative required) will lead more frequently to cheating (copying and downloading);

Graph 5.17 Number of books read during the school year and school grades – 9-12 (2017)

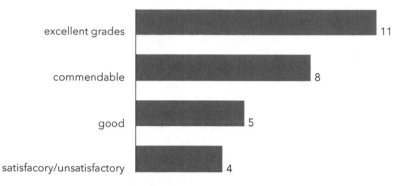

excellent grades	11
commendable	8
good	5
satisfacory/unsatisfactory	4

Source: Czech National Library (base: all)

- that amongst the youngest children a large role is played in the selection of books by the recommendations of parents, while older children are more guided by friends' recommendations;
- that a book has to hold children's interest from the outset, otherwise they have problems reading it;
- that the family background (home library and reading parents) is of key importance for children's reading development;
- that parents should not insist on particular titles that they read when they were young. This often creates a quite large obstacle;
- that strong readers are not bothered by sizeable books, whereas weaker readers prefer smaller books (without descriptions and with gripping plots).

TYPES

Statistics can also show other things besides correlations and trends. Several items can be brought together and interlinked, and their intersections sought, using what is known as cluster analysis. The outcome is several types, which remain at the level of statistics, but which nevertheless show our reading behaviour in a somewhat more three-dimensional way.[68]

Regarding clustering itself: several areas of reading culture are interconnected within it — the areas of reading (i.e. the number of books read, reading in foreign languages, reading frequency, what we are reading, reading magazines, favourite authors and books), digitality (reading on various devices, (dis)agreement that books might only be in electronic form, usage of the internet and what we read on it), media activities, leisure time, acquisitions and the book market (methods, money spent on books, criteria for book purchases, whether or not we have an overview of the book market, why we do not buy books, information on books, book market institutions, home libraries), reader socialization, the relationship between reading and employment and public libraries (whether we visit them, which services we seek in them, how satisfied we are with them, why we do not go to libraries and what other services we would welcome in them). All of this is naturally interconnected with socio-demographic variables (age, education, economic activity, nature of work, income per household member, size of town of residence and area).

1. "I don't read, I don't buy, I'm not interested." (23%).

   This category is conspicuously filled by men with primary education only (those who have completed an apprenticeship), whose media activities primarily include watching TV. They do not even read magazines (or sports magazines only at most); they neither buy nor receive books; they do not go to the library and at home they have fifty books at most.

2. "I enjoy reading, but books are very expensive. The ideal solution is the library." (25%)

   This category is dominated by women aged 60+; education primarily primary (with apprenticeship), economically inactive; they

68   See Jiří Trávníček, *Reading Bohemia. Readers and Reading in the Czech Republic at the Beginning of the 21th Century*, transl. by Melvyn Clarke (Praha: Akropolis - Institute of Czech Literature, CAS, 2015), pp. 69-72.

Graph 5.18 Types (2013)

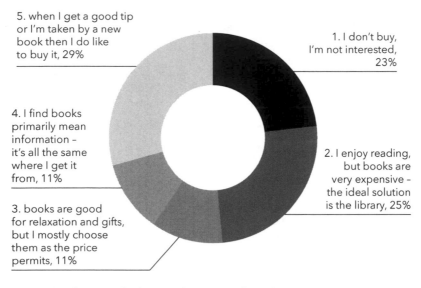

5. when I get a good tip or I'm taken by a new book then I do like to buy it, 29%

1. I don't buy, I'm not interested, 23%

4. I find books primarily mean information – it's all the same where I get it from, 11%

2. I enjoy reading, but books are very expensive - the ideal solution is the library, 25%

3. books are good for relaxation and gifts, but I mostly choose them as the price permits, 11%

Source: Czech National Library and Institute of Czech Literature, CAS (base: 97% of sample)

read books sporadically but read quite a lot of magazines; they stick to printed books; they do not use the internet; their favourite leisure-time activities are gardening and holiday homesteading; they do not buy books, as they find them too expensive; they borrow them to a large extent from friends; they do not have a good overview of what is being published (there is too much); at home they have one hundred books at most; they have always gone and still go to the library; they prefer leisure reading and books on religious subjects.

3. "Books are good for relaxation and gifts, but I mostly choose them as the price permits." (11%)

This is to a large extent a gender-neutral category, relating primarily to people aged 40–50, educated up to secondary level, whose work is half and half (both physical and mental); they read sporadically;

they buy books but generally do not receive them; they do not go to the library, although they used to go; they do not even borrow books from friends; occasionally they do buy a book; they do not have an overview of what is being published; at home they have a hundred books at most; reading is not usually associated with their work; they prefer leisure fiction.

4. "I find books primarily mean information. It's all the same where I get it from." (11%)
   A category that is not gender-specific; graduates (and singles) predominate; they read intensively (often and a lot), and they also read a lot in foreign languages; they are very often online; they use all the modern devices (notebooks, tablets, e-readers and smartphones); online they mostly read discussions and comments; out of all magazines they prefer the specialist ones; they receive books in fairly large quantities; if they buy them they primarily choose them by author, they also have other sources; they go to libraries; they download from the intenet quite often; for them books primarily mean study and work; they have an overview of what is being published; at home they have hundreds of books; they were brought up from an early age to read books; there is a strong association for them between reading and work; they prefer textbooks and reference books, as well as sci-fi and fantasy.

5. "When I get a good tip or I'm taken by a new book then I do like to buy it." (30%)
   Predominantly women educated to secondary or graduate level from higher income categories; they read regularly and a lot; they stick to printed books; out of all magazines they prefer the specialist ones, as well as cultural, special-interest (hobby) and women's magazines; they buy books, primarily based on the recommendations of others, but at the same time they receive considerable quantities of them; they have a good overview of what is being published; they have more than one hundred books in their home libraries; they were brought up to read books from an early age; they read a lot of fiction, as well as non-fiction; they do not go

to the library that often – they prefer buying books to borrowing them; they very often want the latest books; as for library services they would above all welcome authors' forums.

SUMMARY AND CONCLUSIONS

This statistical image shows Czech reading culture as a whole to be stable and fairly strong. The latter fact stems primarily from the number of those engaged in at least minimum activity within it. What is slightly disquieting is the decreasing number of those who visit public libraries, though this is just one of the inevitable outcomes of the digital revolution. Many of the services that were previously associated with libraries are now available from the comfort of your home and your personal computer. However, other data show that Czech reading culture is becoming rather leaner. This can clearly be seen in the increase in the number of people who do not even spend a minute of the day reading (books or magazines). This means that reading is slowly vacating the space of everyday life.

One of the most substantial findings is about the family and its role in reader socialization. Growing up in a favourable reading environment does not necessarily serve as a guarantee that we are going to become habitual readers. However, not having that background always means that we are weighed down in our subsequent life by a cultural deficit, i.e. a handicap that we have to overcome either by our own efforts or with the help of other socializing elements, such as schools, friends and public libraries.

A large German survey in 2009 showed that reading within the family develops children's mental and cognitive faculties – a rather predictable platitude. It also showed that like nothing else, reading reverses the disadvantages of children who were never read to, i.e. nowhere else does the "Matthew effect" ("For whosoever hath, to him shall be given") apply as much as it does here – those who have been given within the family will be given all the more, while those who have not been given will have to make up for that deficit all the more.[69] It also became apparent that interest in reading, once brought to life, will never be subsequently lost. And this interest is only and uniquely awoken by parents as the child's first models.[70]

69   See e.g. Keith E. Stanovich, "Matthew Effect in Reading: Some Consequences of Individual Differences in the Acquisition of Literacy," *Reading Research Quarterly* 21 (Fall 1986), pp. 360–407; online: http://www.keithstanovich.com/Site /Research_on_Reading_files/RRQ86A.pdf [accessed 2020-04-13].
70   See e.g. "Lesesozialisation in der Familie" (2009); online: http://www .lesen-in-deutschland.de/html/content.php?object=journal&lid=923 [accessed 2020-04-04].

6

From the standpoint of reading life-stories

This section will deal with Czech reading culture from within, as it were, homing in far more on those who uphold it, i.e. the readers. We shall shift the focus from the statistical macro-perspective of the last chapter to the micro-perspective of their individual testimonies, gathered over almost six years of research (2009–2015), using reading life-stories (see Appendix 3 for the question list). As for the source, this was formed in the last chapter by a statistical sample made up of 1,500–2,000 respondents, while here it will be a corpus of 138 individual testimonies. Hence we shall be looking more chronologically in depth at the experience of four contemporary generations that have imprinted themselves on individual anonymously collected testimonies. A second perspective will be provided by several key phenomena, i.e. certain points of intersection. In line with the *oral history* tradition we shall henceforth call individual respondents *narrators*. The main interpretational and classifying perspective will be provided by the generations and not by social strata, however much note we take of such attempts.[71] At the same time narrators have been selected

---

71 See e.g. Rolf Engelsing, *Der Bürger als Leser. Lesergeschichte in Deutschland* (Stuttgart: J. B. Metzler, 1973); Martin Fibiger, *Vztah gymnazistů a vysokoškoláků ke knize, čtení a literární výchově* (Ústí nad Labem: Univerzita J. E. Purkyně, 2013); Roman Chymkowski, *Autobiografie lekturowe studentów* (Warszawa: Biblioteka Narodowa, 2011); Jonathan Rose, *The Intelectual Life of the British Working Classes* (New Haven – London: 2010 [2002]); Jost Schneider. *Sozialgeschichte des Lesens. Zur historischen Entwicklung und sozialen Differenzierung der literarischen Kommunikation in Deutschlad* (Berlin – New York: de Gruyter, 2004); Stanisław Siekierski, *Czytania Polaków w XX wieku* (Warszawa: Wydawnictwo Uniwersytetu Warszawskiego, 2000).

from all social strata and town sizes. Moreover and most importantly, people were selected with varying attitudes to reading, i.e. not only those who declared themselves to be lifelong or committed readers, but also those who do not read at all or who only used to read and have now stopped.[72]

THE FOUR GENERATIONS

Radio: These are 65 and older. In the present-day Czech population there are slightly more than one and three-quarter million of them. As for the length of their lives, this is the generation with the largest age span. It might be better to speak of two to three individual generation waves. The oldest ones had completed their formative period (approx. 14–21) before the war or on the cusp of the 1930s and 1940s, while the youngest are from the 1960s. The experience of the war (and the 1948 Communist take-over) shows itself to be the biggest watershed within this generation, as here we can separate off the stratum or perhaps even the intergeneration from the 1960s (1968) – people who were 15–25 years old at the time, while in many respects this stratum partially overlaps with the following generation (the *television* generation). What they have in common is that the great majority are currently now outside the economic cycle. They have raised children, who have now flown the nest; they are grandparents and in some cases even great-grandparents. The February 1948 generation.

These are called the radio generation, based on the dominant medium that accompanied them as they grew up. It is the case for more or less the entire generation that radio is not felt so strongly to be a background medium, i.e. a backdrop to other activities. Both the youngest and the oldest still remember well the signature tunes of cult programmes that started to be broadcast in the early 1960s,

---

72 For more details see Jiří Trávníček, "Reading and Our Life Stories," *Open Cultural Studies* 2 (2018), pp. 591–597; here there is more literature on readers' life-stories and autobiographical narratives.

drawing the attention of the entire audience. As for concurrent usage of radio and television, it is only among this generation that we can note, quite prominently among the males, that they watched sports broadcasts on television with the sound turned off while the radio was turned on, because the commentary there was of a far higher professional standard and a lot more vivid.

Many of them only learnt to handle computers and the internet very late on, and some, particularly the oldest, often gave up completely. They have seen the emergence of numerous media throughout their lives, so they cannot believe that digitality will have any profound consequences. They thought that this way they would only gain a little extra until they eventually had to realize that their lack of computer knowledge and inability to work with the internet was increasingly excluding them from society and even from the society of friends and those closest to them. ("Grandma, send it to me by email." "You'll find it online, Grandad.")

As for their attitude towards reading, there used to be a large cultural difference between the town and the country. A large proportion of this generation come from the village. "Stop reading and go sweep the courtyard instead."; "What are you lounging around here with a book for when there's rabbits to be fed?"; "Have you got nothing better to do than read?" Girls reading were considered particularly unseemly, especially out in the villages. Almanacs are even mentioned as primary written-word sources. Particularly for those who grew up in the country, it was not entirely untypical for them to make their first contact with a book at school. In general this institution played a far greater role in this generation's reader socialization than was the case for any of the younger generations.

Their attitudes towards books are for the most part very earnest, indeed almost reverential. Even those who do not count as strong readers make sure that they treat books with consideration, and indeed in one family the parents are reported to have checked that their children had washed their hands before reading a book. The youngest amongst them were affected by the ideological indoctrination of the

1950s. In many cases they read whatever came to hand, hence the quite considerable role played by "pulp" literature (sugary romances, westerns, cowboy stories and the like). They have the most positive attitude towards reading the Bible, as they are the most religious of all generations, and they have also very much taken to serialized radio readings.

Out of all the generations it is their reading habits that have been exposed to the greatest number of changes and – to put it in present-day language – challenges. Hence their critical views towards the younger and particularly the youngest generations that they do not appreciate books, they read in a disorderly manner, they are always sat in front of a computer and so on. Their attitude towards current book output is mostly restrained and negative: they do not understand it, and they are bothered by its crudity and sexual openness.

Television: They are between 45 and 64. In the present-day Czech population there are slightly more than two and three-quarter million of them. To a large extent this is the generation of the 1960s. Many of them lived through 1968 in their formative years, the oldest sharing their "68-ness" with the youngest strata of the previous generation. The youngest strata of this generation did their growing-up during the "normalization" period. They also lived through the collapse of the Communist regime, which happened at a time when they could still do something with their lives – begin something new or find some new energy within themselves. For those born in the early 1960s this historical period proved to be unfair on two accounts – it did not allow them to experience the 1960s as they entered maturity and in 1989 it did not place them in the role of those behind the changes (as they were no longer students), but only at best as participating observers. The youngest amongst them may be seen as a kind of intergenerational wave from the "soft 1980s", i.e. *perestroika*, the disintegration of Communism, the relaxation of travel restrictions and the rise of alternative activities. They are parents and frequently grandparents.

These are called the television generation. Even the oldest amongst them grew up at a time when television was starting to be the dominant medium both for news and entertainment. During their formative years they witnessed the birth of a second channel (1970) on television here followed by colour broadcasting (1973). The oldest among them had to adapt as the variety of the 1960s turned into the greyness of normalization, but they did indeed get used to it, ignoring the news and the political-ideological programmes and watching mostly sports and serials (such as *Chalupáři* – Cottagers, *Žena za pultem* – Woman Behind the Counter, *Nemocnice na kraji města* – Hospital on the Outskirts of Town). Indeed it was primarily serials that formed the television sensibilities of the television generation.

Many of them actually had their first contact with computers before 1989 on various training courses and visits to more technically proficient friends, but for the most part computer (and subsequently internet) literacy did not get under way for most of them until the fall of the old regime – when computers were no longer an exclusive affair and everybody started to learn their first programs (e.g. the legendary T602 word processor) and to discover over time that a computer could be more than just a "superior typewriter".

They were supposed to be the first generation of "New Humanity", i.e. of those who had only ever been under the sway of Communist institutions. They had grown up under a system of double truths (those expressed at home and in public), which also left its mark on their reading. To a large extent they relied on their parents' home libraries, which often came to be not only an alternative to what was foisted upon them at school, but even a kind of resistanace and opposition. Hence their childhood was largely imbued with the pre-1948 repertoire. A substantial influence was also exercised on their maturation as readers by 1960s literature, which they even managed to make use of under normalization, when some of them got into "unofficial" literature, i.e. samizdat and exile output.

One memorable experience shared by this generation under normalization was that of "Book Thursdays" (see p. 42), which some of them will recall to this day. They often do not understand their children's reading lives and frequently express disappointment that their children have not caught on that much to reading. In general they have a positive attitude to the post-1989 changes, though many of them are overwhelmed by the excessive range of titles. Many of them cannot accept this disenchantment with books, while others have taken it completely for granted. They do not follow contemporary Czech output, particularly fiction, very much, partly because it does not interest them and partly because they are at an age when they are more interested in "real" stories than "fictitious" ones. They have also been impressed by literature in translation – particularly by all the big bestsellers.

Computer: They are between 25 and 44. In the present-day Czech population they come to a total of some three million two hundred thousand. Out of all the four generations presented, they are the most numerous, so here we are dealing with the 1970s population explosion, plus those who were born towards the end of the old regime. Hence this generation includes a kind of semigenerational wave known as "Husák's children". Their formative years were spent on the cusp of the old times and the new, or just slightly afterwards, but most of their lives have taken place since 1989. We might call them the November generation, as they were the ones who – as students or at the age of students – were the main work horses (or rather icons) behind the political changes in 1989. And they were also the ones who managed to profit most from these changes, as the new age opened up for them just at a time when they were spreading their wings in life. Many of them are now parents and the eldest of their children are now themselves flying the family nest.

This is the generation that formed around the cusp of the "old" and the "new" periods. The older ones went through all the Communist educational institutions, while the younger ones only went through some of them. To a large extent we find the same patterns amongst them as in the previous generation, particularly the home/school dichotomy and memories of "Book Thursdays" The youngest also have a lot in common with the internet generation, e.g. their Pottermania and hankering for fantasy. Out of all the generations, this one is most involved in the 1990s.

The computer was already there waiting for them as something unavoidable that brought with it the need to master everything else – the internet and Facebook or other social networks. The older ones amongst them are still more like digital immigrants, while the younger ones are more digital natives. They no longer face the question whether the digital sphere is hostile to the old culture or a rival to it; they simply found that there was nothing else for it but to come to terms with it. They had experienced television at a time when the amount of channels, programmes and broadcasting time was rising in almost geometrical progression. This is the first generation that has to be called *homo zappiens* because of their TV remote controls. Their habits also changed as a result: if I don't like a program then I switch over for half a minute to see if I'll carry on watching. They have also been affected by the advent of various video recorders, so many of them have discovered it is better just to use the television as a screen for recordings from their own video library, while they only switch on television as television for the news or sport. They have learnt far more than those who came before them to only listen to the radio as a background medium early in the morning, at breakfast or in the car.

The book market opened up for them in an unprecedented manner, as did the range of titles on offer and their availability, but at the same time the 1990s became a bit of a trap for them. There was so much that was different, opportunities and challenges, that time for reading inevitably had to be put to one side. This generation is also the one that was most drawn into the maelstrom of the digital revolution. For them it was something new that they had to respond to. Thanks to digitality, many of them learnt an entirely different approach to media than they had been used to in their early years. Of all the generations they made the most of the 1990s reading repertoire – and the new writers that began to emerge at this time. But this new age overwhelmed them so that they frequently have to search for some harmony with it. The generation of the socio-political and digital watershed, just like the generation of new reading waves and names of authors not born until the 1990s.

Internet: They are between 15 and 24. There are about one million two hundred thousand of them in the population. They are the least numerous generation, but that is because their age span only covers one decade, while the other generations cover twenty years. We might call them the internet-Facebook-Twitter-Instagram-YouTube generation, as many of them take Facebook and other social networks to be something quite distinct. We find most of them to be in their formative years, i.e. in the middle of their education, but some have already completed their education and entered the economic cycle.

They were born after the political changes of 1989, so they do not have direct experience of Communist institutions (e.g. school, police, army and other authorities). They would belong to the generation which from a worldwide perspective is called *Generation Z, millennials or pluralists*, i.e. those born during the 1990s. From that global standpoint, few of them come under the previous Generation Y, also called the *echo boom,* the generation of the new millennium.

They were born into digital culture and took it for granted. Hence in contrast to their parents, who are digital immigrants, they did not need to adopt it as another media skill. They live in an age of media glut, which only exacerbates their restlessness. They sit in front of the radio or television to a much lesser extent than their parents did. They are not too interested in the news, and to the extent that they are then they watch it online, either on particular sites or with the aid of what they have found out from friends on social networks. They have practically done away with paper newspapers as digitization has increased. They spend five times more time on Facebook than their parents do. An entirely unique space for them to communicate in is the YouTube network, where many of them have discovered favourite stars and celebrities (a new phenomenon for YouTubers), the kind that are not known on television and thus unknown to other generations. Moreover, these are not just impersonal stars, but they can enter into discussions beneath their videos, write messages to their fans and debate with them on their Facebook profiles.

They live in abundance indeed in superabundance, but they somehow do not seem to appreciate this, perhaps partly because they do not have anything to compare their situation with. The time when their parents used to read out to them as children was not entirely excessive. Their reading culture is not as bad as it is considered by others, e.g. their parents and grandparents. The fact that so many of them receive a secondary and higher education clearly indicates that the "reading follows on behind education" rule no longer applies, and we find grammar school pupils who say they have not read a single book, without being a complete exception within this generation. In previous generations they would be considered to be a phenomenon on the borderline of cultural pathology.

For them reading comes to be far more of an individual choice, a liking and a value preference. It is not associated with social prestige except in well-defined communities. The identifying sign of this generation, i.e. what is truly and uniquely theirs alone, and what they have had the opportunity to live through during their initial phase is the fantasy genre and in particular the Harry Potter series. This often makes them proud that "they were there", i.e. that these books were written primarily for them. They find the boundary between individual media to be quite permeable, i.e. they have come to terms with the transmedia reading pattern. For the most part they appreciate ready availability and user-friendliness, so that surprisingly the classic book frequently wins out over the e-reader and the computer. What kind of prestige does reading enjoy within their generation? In some respects this has not been stabilized, as most of them are still being educated and prepared, as it were, for "real" life, while in other respects it is not substantial. They chat with each other more about films, the internet, Facebook and computer games. This is the *Harry Potter* generation.

PHENOMENA

A total of more than thirty emerged, which can be divided into three groups:

1. authors, genre works: *Babička* (Granny by Božena Němcová), poetry, Betty MacDonald, the Bible, *Broučci* (Beetles by Jan Karafiát), detective stories, *The Egyptian* (by Mika Waltari), Alois Jirásek, Pottermania, compulsory reading, *Švejk* (by Jaroslav Hašek) etc.
2. the institution of reading culture: the home library, public library, region, tipsters, teachers, prohibitions etc.
3. reading strategies (states): returns, unfinished reading, apostasy, auxiliary reading, guilty-pleasure reading, the glut, printed versus electronic books etc.

These phenomena present a kind of map of Czech reading culture and its key footholds. Its landmarks stand out.

Let us now select one phenomenon from each group that is characteristic of Czech reading culture and examine it in greater detail.

BETTY MACDONALD

This is a phenomenon that has long dominated Czech reading culture, particularly its female constituency. Moreover, this phenomenon cannot be found anywhere else. It involves works by *Betty MacDonald,* particularly her autobiographical novel *The Egg and I.*

As regards her popularity in the USA, *The Egg and I* was the eighth biggest non-fiction bestseller in 1945, and a year later it was number one, but then her celebrity waned among both readers and booksellers.[73] However, this was not the case among the Czechs. *The Egg and I.* is an evergreen among readers here, as confirmed by not only our surveys, but also research undertaken by Aleš Haman during the

---

73 See Paula Becker, *Looking for Betty MacDonald. The Egg, the Plague, Mrs. Piggle-Wiggle, add I* (Washington: University of Washington Press, 2016), pp. 67–80.

1980s.[74] If we count up all the votes from all four statistical surveys (2007, 2010, 2013 and 2018), this autobiographical novel still comes out easily on top in the "my favourite book" category.

The Egg and I, a short novel with strong autobiographical elements. This is the simple story of a woman from the big city who moves out with her husband to the country, where they set up a chicken farm together. The woman is confronted by an entirely different environment to the one she had been used to as a town girl. Farmwork and housework are a novelty for her, as are visits to the neighbours, who are people with a totally different mindframe. All of this is described with detachment. The author is not lacking in a sense for everyday observation and a sense of irony that sometimes turns into sardonicism. The rhythm of the book is also assisted by the fresh sequencing of scenes. In a nutshell, something is always going on. *The Egg and I* is classified as humorous prose or autobiography.

What attracts the Czech reader to this book so much? Apparently its humour, particularly the way serious things are described with detachment: "Yes, as for the descriptiveness and the art of making fun then sure, I think I had a good laugh. What I really took away from her was the description of how wayward inanimate objects can be. Is this personification? She is really a past master at this," (female accountant, aged 40). Or more broadly: "The topmost book? For me that is Betty MacDonald and her *The Egg and I*. What I like about her is her view of the world, which she doesn't take tragically. She's an optimist; she can come to grips with it. Her view of adolescents is like marvellous. I've read *The Egg and I* many times. If I don't have anything to read then this is the first thing that I reach for," (female wage accountant, aged 49).

Hence this is a book that offers its readers positive energy. How exactly? "With its view of the world" or "its optimism", as the previous samples say, but perhaps even more so because of its humour. "Mum likes detective stories or comedies like Betty MacDonald and Ivanka

---

74   See Aleš Haman, *Literatura z pohledu čtenářů* (Praha: Československý spisovatel, 1991), particularly pp. 69–81

The Egg and I - cover of the first Czech edition in 1947

Devátá. Not dramas and definitely not classics." (female graphic designer, aged 28). And there is one other important attribute here too, namely the woman's point of view and her ability to portray a woman's lot: "I used to read Betty MacDonald. Why? Because she plays a female tune. Hard graft – no love. That's why women like it. For example, the way she described learning the piano and ballet... and then did nothing but lug buckets of soil and vegetables, while her husband just bellyached at her. The readers will all say wow, I'm not doing so badly, I'm not living like that yet," (female, retired shop assistant, aged 66).

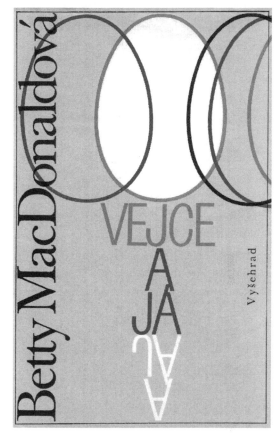

The Egg and I – cover of the sixth Czech edition in 1989 (print run: 99,000 copies)

Characteristically, several of the previous testimonies included references to other points of contact besides merely literary ones. For female Czech readers[75] *The Egg and I* also frequently reflects their own lives, as well as much that is of comfort and encouragement. This might be rather therapeutic reading, but where does the boundary lie between "real" and "therapeutic" reading? Is it not the most powerful

---

75 See also Gordon and Patricia Sabine, *Books That Made the Difference. What People Told Us* (Hamden: Library ofProfessional Publications 1984 [1983]), p. 17; or http://bettymacdonaldfanclub.blogspot.cz/ [accessed 2020-04-06].

books that are most associated with our needs in life, our experiences, crises and shortfalls? These are books that provide strength, i.e. books in which the boundary between the Kantian self-objective of aesthetic pleasure and "the other" becomes blurred. All in all, this combination of humour and fortification, opinion and personal credo is expressed by the following narrator:

> What I regret is that I never got to know her [Betty] alive, when I could have written to her. If I'd been able I'd have written to her straight away, because of the affinity that I feel towards her, and I'd have thanked her for all the people she delighted with her books. In America they don't even know her while here in this country she has a lot of readers and her humour is close to our heart. They have a different sense of humour. I would also have written to her that her books provided me with strength at a difficult time when I was looking after my ailing mother. (retired female teacher, aged 74).

To summarize, Betty MacDonald offers reading that is helpful and fortifying. Moreover, her books have a certain Czech emancipation, and not just for their readers, as they offer a female hero who can hold her own in a man's world with her own weapons, even though they are not always typically women's weapons.

HOME LIBRARIES

Here we often come across something resembling foundational fervour, or to be specific, the idea that the narrator's parents were the first generation to start building up their own library: "My parents had a library at home, but they created it themselves. They did not have any books from their own parents. Dad had only been to primary school, but he had natural intelligence, and he used to go foraging for books, while mum wanted to be a teacher, and she enjoyed school too, but they didn't have any money for books when she was young. They might only have had what they borrowed." (female, retired pensioner, aged 70). Not infrequently the moment is remembered when books first appeared at home as the parents bought them or inherited them from their parents: "Dad was one of three children. He was a trained fitter, but he did various other jobs. Like my grandfather he was a bookworm, and he inherited his library (with around seven hundred books)." (male, a self-employed trader, aged 46). The parents' library becomes a place of intellectual exploration, often with the purpose of somehow penetrating alien territory:

> When I learnt to read I used to scour through my parents' library. [...] When I was in about the seventh year of school I discovered Mácha's Máj.[76] It was probably the first book that I found totally enchanting, as it both terrified and attracted me. I had found it in my parents' library. I used to read a lot about infectious diseases, because dad was a doctor, so we did have something at home after all, but I did rummage out that Mácha. I remember it as ecstasy. I do not ever recall having such an amazing feeling while reading poetry as I had then (male secondary biology teacher, aged 50).

Hence the presence of a home library provides not only security and convenience for the reader (as there is no need to hunt for books elsewhere), but it also sets a task for the future when the narrator becomes independent: "One day I would like to have my own library with all that real seminal world literature. I'm now trying to stick something like that together. That's kind of my dream," (female secondary veterinary vocational college student, aged 18). This can sometimes involve something like *l'art pour l'art* or – to put it less positively – a fetish: "I am programmatically building up a library – I'm hoarding books. I won't ever read them, but I carry on building it," (male secondary school history teacher, aged 37).

In the Czech setting, a home library even acts as a kind of citadel that helps you to survive bad times such as in our case the Protectorate (1939-1945) and forty years under the Communists (1948-1989).

---

76 Karel Hynek Mácha: *Máj* (May, 1836), a lyrical-epic work, the most iconic Czech poetry book.

Here they could find titles from the First Republic and books that were excluded from public libraries in the early1950s and then the early 1970s. This way many people could gain access to a collection from the 1960s later under normalization.

One narrator (the 50-year-old male secondary school biology teacher) talks of his home library as an "external intelligence" or as something that enables him to be independent, even of the public library, which from his standpoint is time-consuming (he often has to wait several months for books) or elsewhere: "I don't go to the library. I make do with my own resources," (retired male chemist, aged 67). The value of home libraries increases in line with external political and social conditions. In recent times the internet (and indeed digitality as a whole) has deprived them of considerable weight, but even so a certain reflex can be observed in the Czech population involving thinking of worse times and stocking up and entrenching oneself for when they come.

Perhaps home libraries play a greater role than the Czechs are willing to admit, and not only as part of reading culture. Apart from the social (a link) and cultural (a citadel in times of siege) aspects, there is also an educational element (an educational institution). Its very presence can have a certain influence. By always being on view, books become something to be taken for granted.

GLUT

In reading terms the Czech population went hungry under the Communists, particularly with regard to popular titles and their limited print-runs. At the time such rhetorical questions could now be heard as "Will there be enough books for everyone this year? Without queueing? Will we see the end of that enraging situation where you have to run around a dozen bookshops in vain?"[77] Books were

---

77 František Lukáš, "Úvaha o literatuře tzv. nedostatkové," *Kulturní tvorba* 3 (1965), no. 8, p. 8.

a scarce, under-the-counter commodity with what was known as a "narrow profile". Then came the post-1989 era when the question had to be turned round completely: "Where is it all going lead if an average of fifty books are published *every day*?" Indeed "books are in total overproduction here," reports publisher Filip Tomáš;[78] another publisher Juraj Heger seconds him: "readers are disorientated," [79] bookstore chain owner Jan Kanzelsberger adds his voice: "We have got ourselves into a situation where the supply is killing demand"[80]; and geologist Václav Cílek says that the quantity of books that is barraging down on us "is flustering and disturbing".[81] "The frequency of new publications is too frantic," former editor-in-chief of the Odeon publishers Jiří Pelán grumbles,[82] expressing the generally shared complaint that nowadays the shelf life of books has grown shorter, particularly that of new works.

It was primarily the oldest generation who lived through a reading famine. Books (and everything else to read) were very scarce during their childhood, particularly out in the countryside. "There wasn't the money. Although dad was earning, we just had a little cottage and we were saving up for a bigger one. We didn't buy many books," (a retired seamstress and home worker, aged 92). Many of them did not come across their first book until they went to school: "We didn't have any books at home to read. I didn't start reading until I was at school," (retired male design engineer, aged 73). Buying books was definitely not a frequent habit but rather something special: "When I was small our parents didn't buy us books, but clothes – dresses

---

78   Cited from Petra Sýkorová, "Když nabídka likviduje poptávku," *Profit* 21 (2010), no. 14, p. 20.

79   Juraj Heger, "Knihy levnější být nemůžou " interview by Petra Tesařová, *Lidové noviny* 22. 3. 2011, p. 14.

80   Cited from Petra Sýkorová, "Když nabídka likviduje poptávku" cited article, p. 20.

81   Václav Cílek, "Zneklidňující množství knih," interview by Svatava Antošová, *Tvar* 22 (2011), no 3, p. 4.

82   Cited from Jiří Trávníček, *Překnížkováno. Co čteme a kupujeme* (2013) (Brno-Praha: Host-Czech National Library, 2014), p. 30.

and that," (retired female farm worker and pastry cook, aged 71). A book was a rarity, so they very carefully cut out serialized novels which they then had bound. Many grew up believing that reading and books were just for libraries and schools. Other duties awaited them at home.

The Communist period was a time of scarcity: the book-hungry demand lacked any matching supply, see "Book Thursdays" and the legendary queues that formed for books. Those most in demand often disappeared within a couple of hours and were not available again. Considering the inflexibility of production at that time, this meant that the reader went without the title in question. Then came the breakthrough.

"There was a flood of books at the cusp of the old and the new regimes. We bought masses of books," (female doctor, aged 61). Indeed other people also recall that moment when the books started to mass up in the early 1990s. Habits from the previous age died hard in many of us, e.g. "if I don't buy it now then I never will." The oldest generation in particular did not know how to handle this, as books had wielded a huge power over them throughout their childhood and youth inter alia because of their rarity and unavailability, so that then in their maturity there were rather too many books. Many reflect this contradiction in their testimonies: "There wasn't much choice. It wasn't like today when there's a glut, I'd say," (retired male locksmith and repairman, aged 74).

For many there was a culture shock and proof that the availability of a book need not be perceived as just a positive thing. Let us also have a look at the free depositions of respondents from the last statistical survey (2013). Complaints over the excessive supply, in which it was hard to find one's bearings, appear in the testimonies of all the generations: "So many books are published these days that ordinary people cannot find their way around," (woman, aged 50–59); "There are lots of titles on the market – I can't get my bearings in all that very well," (man, aged 40–49); "The book market is overwhelmed by mediocre literature," (man, aged 50–59); "The book market is flooded – with cookbooks and various silliness from actors and similar celebrities," (man, aged 15–19), "A lot of trash is being published," (woman, aged 20–29).

Sometimes surprise is expressed at how so many books can be economically sustainable: "So it seems to me that there's quite an excess of new books, but I don't know. Maybe it all works out somehow, even in today's price conditions," (male IT technician, aged 63). Or here is a more subtle view: "But it's true that as so much is being brought out, I give up straight away on being able to get some kind of coherent overview," (male historian and archaeologist, aged 47). Or even more nuanced: "We have an overload of Danielle Steele, detective stories and horror stories, but what I find missing on the book market and perhaps also in the selection and acquisition of books at this library is the social novel," (male system programmer, aged 66). So despite the glut and overload there is still something missing here. The question arises, however, whether this complaint is primarily addressed to the market or to individual writers, particularly those who are not writing the kind of literature that this narrator considers desirable.

Some kind of reliable guide needs to be found in this deluge of books because for the most part people rely on the opinions of those closest to them: "Books do not seem expensive to me now. What does strike me is that there are lots of books and you lose sight of the right ones in amongst all of that. I look for the books that have been recommended by friends," (male information science college student, aged 25). "Perhaps the best advertisement is always a recommendation made by somebody that you know, or an interesting topic," (male historian and archaeologist, aged 47).

It can be said in summary that this phenomenon provides us with both good news and bad news. First the good news. Complaints over the excessive amount of books have been heard ever since books were books. This means that it is not possible to set some objective boundary on what we are and are not able to culturally absorb. The bad news is that the surfeit which causes this glut is at present truly felt to be something very real. It dissipates our attention, shortens books' shelf lives, deprives publishers of their ability to prepare books more soberly and thoughtfully, and for writers, particularly contemporary ones, it creates a tremendous scrum when they realize that the competitive pressure to which they are exposed has never been so great in all the history of Czech reading.

SUMMARY AND CONCLUSIONS

Readers' life-stories show Czech reading culture to be spread quite broadly over four generations with a spectrum of key phenomena. This is due in part to historical experience (i.e. our turbulent 20th century history). The oldest narrators go back to their experience in the 1920s and 1930s, while the youngest only go back to the period following the social and political changes of 1989. The longest period was that of the Communist regime (1948–1989). Only a small proportion of the population (the very youngest) remained unaffected by its institutions, including those which make up part of reading culture. From the perspective of personal experience, however, the period under the Communists is not seen any differently that it is from the standpoint of "history with a big H". Even from that perspective books were passed from hand to hand and strategies were sought to gain access to those which were not in public circulation. Self-help networks were formed or one read whatever came to hand.

One key piece of information that emerges from readers' life-stories is the strongly personal approach to reading, which to some extent involves a duel between experience and aesthetics (of literature). Readers' life-stories include far more situations where reading was somehow of assistance and affected us. This way we find that strong and committed reading stems more from *purposes* than from *contents*. In this light the saying "tell me what you are reading, and I will tell you who you are" proves to be rather misleading or at least incomplete. If we want to find out what impresses a reader and how, we should instead say "tell me why you are reading, and I will tell you who you are." Personal reading is reading with a purpose, or in other words: titles, topics, authors and genres come to life within the framework of autobiographical questioning far more from the vantage point of purposes and motivations than otherwise.

7

From a comparative standpoint

This chapter will compare Czech reading culture with those elsewhere. It will also occasionally make comparisons on the edge of the possible, placing data from surveys of different kinds side by side. Hopefully, this will not be too unfair at least as an illustration of the situation (with its main highlights).[83] As for book market data, this is traditionally understood to be rather unreliable and sometimes even suspect (e.g. in the case of China), and likewise it is not always possible to obtain the very latest data. In any case we shall select data from the recent past. Moreover this will be data from before the coronavirus crisis, which considerably shook the book market throughout the world in 2020, clearly threatening small markets, which are more vulnerable, i.e. more exposed to fluctuations, far more than large markets.

THE BOOK MARKET

In terms of total world population, the Czech Republic makes up about 0.14%, which in terms of book market turnover comes to around 0.25% and in terms of the number of books around 1.4%. Thus we see that its output of titles is ten times higher than the number of inhabitants would indicate. And if we compare the second and the third figures we see that the annual book market turnover is almost five times lower than it ought to be based on the number of titles.

---

[83] See Stephanie Kurschus, *European Book Cultures. Diversity as a Challenge* (Wiesbaden: Springer VS, 2015).

Now let us have a look at national book markets in terms of their volume (annual turnover).

Table 7.1   Six largest book markets

	country	annual turnover (EUR billions)	percentage share of world output
1.	USA	35.0	28.7
2.	China	20.9	14.0
3.	Germany	9.3	7.6
4.	United Kingdom	6.1	5.0
5.	Japan	5.7	4.7
6.	France	3.9	3.2
	Czech Republic	0.3	0.25
x	**World (estimate)**	**122**	**100%**

Source: International Publishers Association and Global Trends in Publishing (2014, 2017, 2018)

Hence in terms of turnover the Czech book market is about one hundred times smaller than the American market, about thirty times smaller than the German market and around ten times smaller than the French market; on the other hand it is around five times larger than the Slovak market. Moreover, this is a market with very small export opportunities – the only country where Czech books are sold in statistically significant numbers is Slovakia.

Another characteristic feature of the Czech book market is its low monopolization, i.e. the small proportion of "big players" in overall output: the five largest Czech publishers control 20% of the market (seven years ago it was 12%), whereas in France it is around 78%, in Holland 75% and in Finland 72%.[84]

---

84   However, this only involves large concerns that bring together several publishing brands; in the Czech Republic this only applies to the two largest – Albartros Media and Euromedia.

The following table shows individual countries in terms of the number of titles published per million inhabitants.

Table 7.2 Number of titles published per million inhabitants

	country	number
1.	United Kingdom	2,875
2.-3.	Taiwan	1,831
2.-3.	Slovenia	1,831
4.-5.	Czech Republic	1,642
4.-5.	Spain	1,626
6.	Georgia	1,547
7.	Norway	1,275
8.	Germany	1,156
9.	France	1,008
10.	Italy	1,000

Source: International Publishers Association, Czech National Library (2012–2018)

The primacy of the United Kingdom in this respect is not surprising, particularly in view of the fact that this country publishes books for practically the entire world and publishes them in the number one global language. Hence this is a market with almost unlimited opportunities, which is still growing, while fully aware that it is not the only country that is publishing in a top global language. Taiwan has China behind it with 1.4 billion inhabitants, i.e. a country that provides fine opportunities for sales (albeit not entirely free politically). Spain is a similar case, with only 49 million inhabitants, but with access to Latin America thanks to its language. Around 2010 the experts even agreed that "Latin America has saved the Spanish publishing industry" (Rüdiger Wischenbart)[85]. Germany, France and Italy are large traditional European markets with well established infrastructures

---

85 Rüdiger Wischenbart,"E book 2018." Interview by Chris Kenneally; online: https://beyondthebookcast.com/wp-content/uploads/2018/12 /WischenbartEBooksAct2Transcript.pdf [accessed 2019-05-10].

and in the first two cases with languages that are spoken in other countries. However, these are also markets that no longer have too many opportunities for expansion.[86]

The book market also involves those who buy books. Let us now have a look at the age distribution of purchasers in the Czech Republic and the USA, even though they differ considerably in terms of size, historical development and the ways in which their markets are organized, so that it is all the more enticing to seek out the conformities and the differences within the socio-demographic sphere. The data is from surveys performed in 2007.

Table 7.3 USA and the Czech Republic – book purchasers by age

	CR	USA
15-24	18%	5%
25-34	20%	11%
35-44	18%	17%
45-54	19%	23%
55-64	11%	21%
65+	14%	23%
total	100%	100%

Source: National Endowment for the Arts, Czech National Library – Institute of Czech Literature, CAS (base: those who buy books)

As can be seen, the work horse of the book market in the Czech population is the *middle generation*, i.e. the older younger and the middle generations, while in the USA it is the older generation, i.e. the older middle and older generations. The greatest differences between the Czech Republic and the USA lie in the *youngest* age cohort (13%).

---

86   See also Angus Phillips – Michael Bhaskar (eds.), *The Oxford Handbook of Publishing* (Oxford – New York: Oxford University Publishing Press, 2019), particularly pp. 207–225 and 399–408.

American data have more of a cumulative nature. The youngest age buys little, those in middle age buy a middling amount and those in old age buy a lot. In contrast the Czech curve shows much greater dependence on economic activity: most books are bought in middle age, i.e. at the peak of our economic career, with fewer in our youngest age and fewest in our old age, when the period of economic activity comes to an end. In this period, as we know from other data, people move to a far greater extent to public libraries.

PUBLIC LIBRARIES

The first table shows the density of public libraries, i.e. the number of inhabitants per library. This data is from 2013 to 2015.

The Czech Republic comes out on top of these countries and clearly worldwide too, which is chiefly thanks to the Libraries Act of 1919 (see p. 37), which set up this network. The network then managed to survive all the subsequent regimes intact, although we have recently witnessed a gradual decline in the number of libraries (see p. 62).

Now let us contrast this criterion of the number of inhabitants per library with another criterion – the number of employees per library.

Inevitably, the denser the network of libraries the smaller the number of employees. A comparison of the two graphs also provides information on the size of the libraries: on the one hand a sparse network of large libraries (as in Lithuania and Portugal) and on the other hand a dense network of small libraries (as in Slovakia and the Czech Republic). Clearly, the automation and robotization processes that have now gathered pace in public libraries (particularly in Scandinavia) are going to reduce the number of employees, or not so much reduce them as move them into other services (e.g. information provision and more personalized relations with public library visitors).

Let us now compare Czech libraries and those in Germany, with its culture that is both historically and geographically close to the Czech

Graph 7.1 Number of inhabitants per public library – several countries

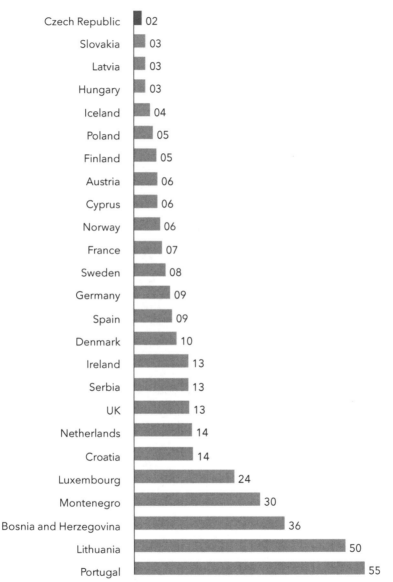

Czech Republic | 02
Slovakia | 03
Latvia | 03
Hungary | 03
Iceland | 04
Poland | 05
Finland | 05
Austria | 06
Cyprus | 06
Norway | 06
France | 07
Sweden | 08
Germany | 09
Spain | 09
Denmark | 10
Ireland | 13
Serbia | 13
UK | 13
Netherlands | 14
Croatia | 14
Luxembourg | 24
Montenegro | 30
Bosnia and Herzegovina | 36
Lithuania | 50
Portugal | 55

Source: Knowledge and Information Centre Eblida

Graph 7.2 Number of employees per public library – several countries[87]

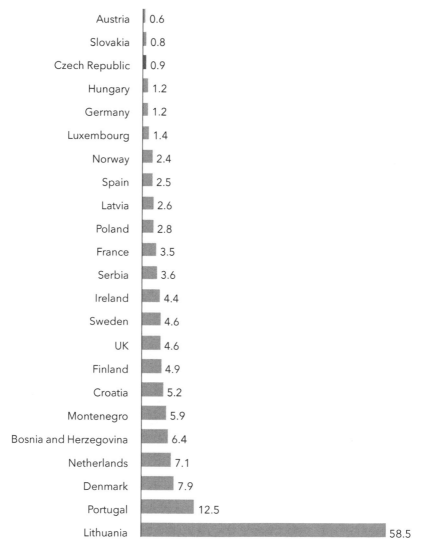

Austria	0.6
Slovakia	0.8
Czech Republic	0.9
Hungary	1.2
Germany	1.2
Luxembourg	1.4
Norway	2.4
Spain	2.5
Latvia	2.6
Poland	2.8
France	3.5
Serbia	3.6
Ireland	4.4
Sweden	4.6
UK	4.6
Finland	4.9
Croatia	5.2
Montenegro	5.9
Bosnia and Herzegovina	6.4
Netherlands	7.1
Denmark	7.9
Portugal	12.5
Lithuania	58.5

Source: Knowledge and Information Centre Eblida

---

87 Cyprus is missing here.

milieu. In this case we can do without data and just work with what was indicated by the data, all on the basis of a single survey.[88]

- German libraries offer users a library collection that is twice to three times smaller than that of Czech libraries;
- German libraries spend around twice more than Czech libraries on their book collection purchases;
- the library collections of German libraries are used about a third more;
- the number of physical visitors to German libraries and Czech libraries is about the same;
- Czech libraries have twice to three times more staff available than German libraries;
- the frequency of visits during opening hours is about 100% higher in German libraries than in Czech libraries;
- operational costs in German libraries are around 100% higher than in Czech libraries;
- Czech libraries arrange twice to three times more cultural and educational events than German libraries.

What does all this mean? Basically that the main strength of Czech libraries is their dense network, which facilitates organization of mutually independent local events. While the dense network is to a large extent also a reason for underfunding, which can particularly be seen in the fact that books are accumulated in libraries even though there is no interest in them among readers. In short, Czech libraries are not there to satisfy readers' demands, and so they find themselves in a vicious circle: users' interest in some of them is decreasing, mainly because they do not replenish their collections – and because public interest is declining, libraries receive less from their founders, which is why they do not replenish their collections.

---

88 Vít Richter, "Benchmarking knihoven a německý Bibliothekindex." In Marie Šedá (ed.), *Knihovna pro všechny* (Ostrava: Moravskoslezská vědecká knihovna, 2015), pp. 6-24; online: https://katalog.svkos.cz/exlibris/aleph/a22_1/apache _media/337UYS77J2KQXBFLLA9EVR2YEIN667.pdf [accessed 2020-04-06].

READING AND READERSHIP

The following table presents data from representative EU research (Eurobarometer). This involved a survey into nine cultural activities, one of which was reading. The question concerned focused on the frequency of reading, and the information in the table also shows those who had at least read a book once over the past twelve months. A total of 25,000 respondents (15+) took part, answering face-to-face in their homes (using their mother tongue).

The first information more or less corresponds to the data from our first research; the second information (i.e. the fall to 72%) comes from outside our data. In order to be able to interpret this difference, we would need to know something about the design of the European survey and what was behind it. In any case the Czech Republic came just below the top in the first survey, while it was above average in the second.

The data clearly shows a north-south axis, which derives both from the social structure (those in the north have a higher overall level of education) and from historical factors. Whereas Sweden has been almost fully literate since the end of the 18th century, Portugal still had 10% illiteracy in the early 1990s (mostly in the villages). A role is also played by the climate and the ensuing lifestyles that separate northerners from southerners.

In the following section let us look at some individual aspects of reading culture by making several comparisons.

This data is from a survey taken in 2010, with the criteria for readers being identical in both cases – one book read in the course of a year.

Let us now compare indices not in terms of performance but from a socio-demographic standpoint. It turns out that in both cases the gender difference is almost identical – in favour of women; in Czech reading culture it is proportionally somewhat greater. However, the age category also shows great differences. Whereas we see a fall in the 30–39 age cohort on the Czech scale, the Polish scale shows a slight decline only: the older the inhabitants the less they read. Both indices also cover education, as it is the case both in Poland and the

Table. 7.4 Readers in the EU (2007 and 2013)

	2007	2013	difference
Sweden	87%	91%	+4%
Netherlands	85%	86%	+1%
Denmark	83%	82%	-1%
United Kingdom	82%	80%	-2%
Germany	82%	79%	-3%
Estonia	79%	78%	-1%
Luxembourg	72%	76%	+4%
Ireland	77%	75%	-2%
Finland	79%	75%	-4%
Austria	79%	74%	-5%
France	71%	73%	-2%
Latvia	75%	73%	-2%
Czech Republic	82%	72%	-10%
Slovenia	72%	68%	-4%
Slovakia	81%	68%	-13%
Lithuania	65%	67%	+2%
Belgium	64%	65%	+1%
Spain	59%	61%	+2%
Hungary	78%	60%	-12%
Bulgaria	59%	56%	-3%
Italy	59%	56%	-3%
Cyprus	57%	56%	-1%
Malta	46%	56%	+10%
Poland	65%	56%	-9%
Croatia	X[89]	56%	X
Romania	61%	52%	-9%
Greece	59%	51%	-8%
Portugal	51%	40%	-9%
EU-27	72%	68%	-4%

Source: Eurobarometer (base: each country approx. 1,000 respondents)

---

89   Not surveyed that year (Croatia was not yet a EU member).

Graph 7.3 The Czech Republic and Poland - breakdown of readers

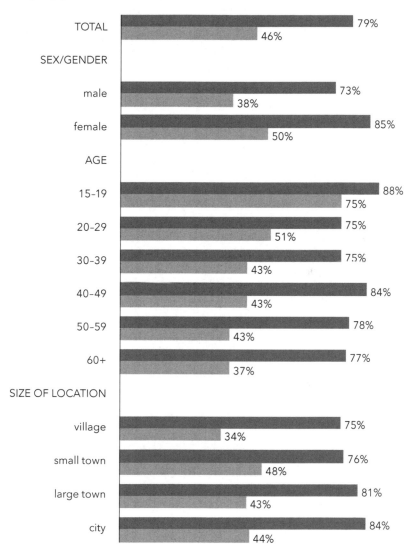

TOTAL — 79% / 46%

SEX/GENDER

male — 73% / 38%

female — 85% / 50%

AGE

15-19 — 88% / 75%

20-29 — 75% / 51%

30-39 — 75% / 43%

40-49 — 84% / 43%

50-59 — 78% / 43%

60+ — 77% / 37%

SIZE OF LOCATION

village — 75% / 34%

small town — 76% / 48%

large town — 81% / 43%

city — 84% / 44%

■ Czech Republic   ■ Poland

Source: Polish National Library, Czech National Library – Institute of Czech Literature, CAS (base: all)

Czech Republic that the older the inhabitants, the lower the level of their education. However, the Czech data does not fully confirm this association. What is more characteristic is the decline between the first two age cohorts, i.e. around the time we enter the economic cycle. The two scales come closest to each other in the youngest cohort, clearly due to pragmatic factors (i.e. school and education) which can compel us to read: "we read because we have to".

As for the size of the town of residence, the Czech data only show a slight trend towards urbanization – i.e. the larger the town, the larger the number of readers (though other surveys do not show this so prominently), while the Polish data is characterized by a large difference between the town and the village. Even the data in this category is something of a disguised index of education, as fewer graduates live in the (Czech and·Polish) villages than in the towns. However, the Polish village shows an entirely different cultural model than the Czech village. The former involves a difference of degree while the latter involves a difference of scale, while the Polish "otherness" is not so much the result of a different socio-cultural model as its *amorphous nature*,[90] i.e. the absence of any model at all. Not reading – as we know (see p. 94) – is not an attitude but the lack of an attitude.

Hence amongst other things reading points towards a society's *esprit de corps*. The larger the differences between the individual socio-demographic categories, the lower the social cohesion. Hence in the Polish environment reading becomes far less of an important social denominator than in the Czech environment. Also noteworthy is the figure showing the overall number of readers. While this survey (2010) indicates that it does not come to one half on the Polish side (and in subsequent surveys it falls to almost one third), it comes to four fifths on the Czech side. What does this mean? It means that in

---

90 See Katarzyna Wolff, *Książka w społecznej przestrzeni polskiej wsi* (Warszawa: Biblioteka Narodowa, 2008).

Poland reading ceases to be not just a socially prestigious activity but also a majority activity, i.e. one that is taken for granted socially.

There are also historical reasons involved. As these modern-era states were coming into being (1918), the situations in both of them with regard to literacy were quite different. The Czech lands were already fully literate while Poland was still confronting enormous illiteracy – under the Russians it was over one half, under the Austrians it was about a third and under the Prussians it was around five percent. Hence a state entity emerged with huge differences and with a large cultural burden that was only successfully eliminated after the Second World War, even though, despite the huge wave of industrialization and urbanization, it was still a country with a large peasantry. As the data indicate, the Polish village was always unable to extricate itself from its socio-cultural "doom" – as a place for the old and the least educated.

In our comparison of the Czech and Polish situations, let us also continue in the following graph, which shows the intensity of

Graph 7.4 The Czech Republic and Poland - number of books read per year

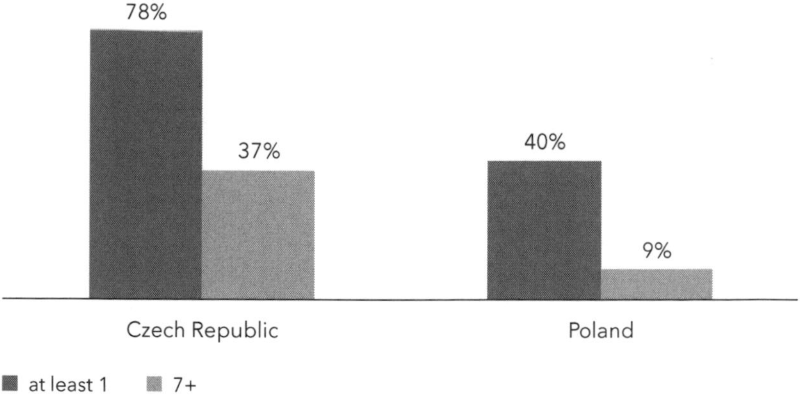

Source: Polish National Library, Czech National Library – Institute of Czech Literature, CAS (base: all)

reading, i.e. the number of those who have read one and seven books per year. In both cases the data are from a survey taken in 2018.

It turns out that the Czech reading rate "seven and more books per year" approximately matches the Polish reading rate "at least one book per year". Whereas in terms of statistical readers (at least one book) we are dealing with a ratio of 2:1 in favour of Czech reading culture, in the case of regular readers (seven and more books) the ratio is approximately 4.5:1, so that here Poland is lacking not only a basic cultural standard but also to a far greater extent a reading elite, i.e. the work horses of reading culture. We have actually attempted a further comparison, which indicated that the level of Czech reading as

Graph 7.5 How many volumes were in my home library when I was 16? – 15 countries

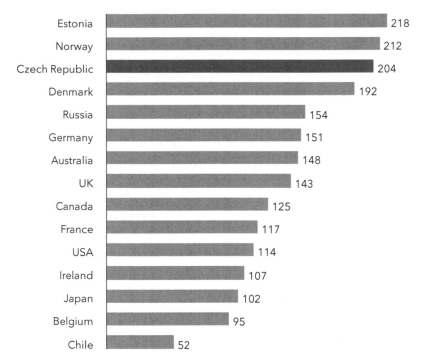

Source: World Reading Habits (2018)

a whole ("at least one book a year") matches the level on the Polish side of graduates over forty.

The most important reading culture socialization environment is the family, and a home library is all part of a family, as the very presence of books in our homes involves indirect socialization. Let us look at this phenomenon from two angles. The first graph includes data from World Reading Habits (2018); in the second one the German data is from a 2008 survey and the Czech data is from a 2010 survey.

We do not know on which basis these countries were selected, but here too the predominance of the north (to which in cultural terms the Czech Republic also belongs) is also made clear.

Graph 7.6   The Czech Republic and Germany - size of home libraries (number of volumes)

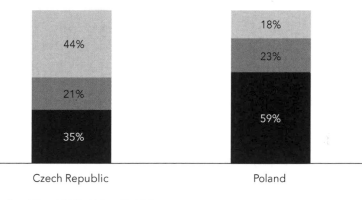

Czech Republic   Poland

■ less than 50   ■ 50-100   ▨ 100+

Source: Stiftung Lesen and Czech National Library – Institute of Czech Literature, CAS (base: all)

The home libraries of three fifths of the population of Germany average out at 50 volumes, while a little more than one third of the Czech population show the same figure. At the opposite end less than one fifth of the population of Germany indicate home libraries with more than 100 volumes, while the same figure is reported by over two fifths of the Czech population.

There is a historical reason behind this. Czech home libraries are still to a large extent multi-generational, i.e. they have been handed down, which to some extent explains their greater size. A home library (see p. 110) was a storehouse for lean times, i.e. times when works by certain authors were withdrawn from public circulation by the censors, a situation that has been repeated a total of three times over the past quarter century – under the German occupation (1939–1945), in the early 1950s and in the early 1970s. In many cases home libraries, especially the larger, well-kept ones, operated as a resource for a broad network of acquaintances and relatives. In contrast, libraries in German households were built up in a far more utilitarian manner, i.e. not as storehouses for worse times or as "educational strongholds".

In conclusion let us submit Czech reading culture to an overall comparison involving inter alia the data presented above.

What does reading culture in the Czech Republic have in common with reading in other countries (particularly in Western cultures)?
- the level of education attained as the main differentiating factor: the higher it is, the stronger is the reading
- the difference between individual generations with regard to reading in a digital environment and online book purchasing – the older we are, the lower our share

How does reading culture in the Czech Republic differ from reading culture in other countries?
- there is a greater difference between men and women (in favour of women)
- the size of the town only plays a minor role
- the age category does not play a major role
- home libraries are large and widespread
- it is customary to see books as presents

- there is a relatively large number of people who visit public libraries
- there is a relatively large number of passionate readers, i.e. those who read more than 50 books a year.

SUMMARY AND CONCLUSIONS

A comparative view shows Czech reading culture to be quite strong in terms of performance indices. Its densest network of public libraries in the world is its great strength, but that is a double-edged sword, because the density of the network is also highly demanding on financial maintenance (replenishment of the collection and equipment). However, another advantage is that it provides facilities for broad cultural activities that are not necessarily directly associated with books and reading, e.g. cultural and educational events.

In terms of performance the Czech book market is also in very good shape, particularly with regard to the ratio of published titles to number of inhabitants. However, this too is double-edged. This market, which is among the smaller ones and has nowhere else to expand, can only afford such quantities of titles at the price of constant "overheating". This means the moment has to come when it cools down or undergoes greater rationalization, as this pace can only be maintained by more and more growth, which leads to an increase in the number of publications, which inevitably shortens the time for their preparation. The second route consists in only publishing guaranteed bestsellers, i.e. books that are already known to be commercial successes for publishers and booksellers. However, this route leads to impoverishment of the range on offer and above all to the elimination of minority genres and authors who are not yet established. Hence some balance between culture and business needs to be sought.

As for reading, Czech reading culture does not in any way show high socio-demographic thresholds apart from those we also find elsewhere – for sex/gender and education. Its advantage is the low

urbanization barrier (the size of the town does not play any substantial role), as well as the age factor. There are also other strong
socialization elements – with widespread use of home libraries (by
98% of the adult population) and the customary perception of books
as presents.

8
From the participants' and experts' standpoints

In this chapter we would like to present a review of all those involved in Czech reading culture and those who are amongst its specialist observers: e.g. the publishers, librarians, writers and anybody engaged in the promotion of reading. The question was worded: "How does present-day Czech reading culture look to you? And everything to do with reading and books? Where do you see its strong and weak points? And where is it heading?"

VIEWS AND STANDPOINTS

Women. Those who uphold reading culture most in this country are clearly the women. They read more, they buy more books, they go to the World of Books and other events more and above all they discuss books more ("personally" even on social networks). One only has to look at any discussion group on books to see the women there on a power play. They are also behind the great majority of reading-club style activities and the like.

Young adult. A constantly neglected phenomenon in this country. Specialists overlook this category, and its English name in Czech is a constant irritant, so attempts are made to get it translated as *literatura pro mládež* ("literature for youth"). However, *young adult* is a specific type of literature with its own rules and subgenres. Thanks to its appealing and distinctive covers and the general marketing approach of its publishers, it is reproached for "tawdriness", although this cannot be said of the "young adult" category as a whole. I would insist that "young adult" is the salvation of literature. In previous decades if teenagers read then they did not particularly boast about it. During breaktime they were not dealing with books, but game levels, new episodes of serials, rappers' albums and Hollywood films. But *Young Adult* is sexy. This kind of literature does not confront pop culture and show-business but quite the reverse, it works together with them very closely, making use of their approaches.

Libraries. The academic community is of course well aware of the importance of libraries, but this dense, well-organized and very active network is very much taken for granted in the popular consciousness. Even for a person from the profession it is surprising just how many libraries are active organizing various events and activities. If publishers did not look down their noses a bit at them (as they take sales away from them after all), they could use them to help create bestsellers, and if the politicians knew more about them they could use them to help win elections.

RADOVAN AUER,
Director of the World of Books trade fair

The Czech language, and by extension books in that language, have from the historical perspective come to form the foundation on which our nation has survived alongside much larger and more powerful neighbours. We carry this from one generation to the next despite the changing circumstances. In comparison with other countries reading culture here is at a high standard and has relatively high prestige. However, nothing lasts forever and there is always something to work on. I believe that everything depends on the three imprescriptible mainstays: family, school and a cultural institution, normally the library.

I primarily see the negative side in the broad range of titles on offer – the high-standard, average and decidedly kitsch that have appeared on our book market practically unfiltered with no substantial sorting or qualified assessment (sporadic reviews in the press are no solution). New and inexperienced readers without any guidance from adults, particularly parents, teachers and perhaps libraries are then at the mercy of quite brutal assaults from powerful publishers, whose interests are primarily economic and not the development of reading culture. I see another risk in the glamour of unrestricted access to new audiovisual media and communications networks that not only narrow down and flatten the range of new books on offer, but to a large extent detract from book reading.

I trust in the ever-strong tradition of the positive attitude towards reading and readership in this country for subsequent developments. But this should not be left entirely to chance. The lament is quite often heard that children read less today. I do not think this is absolutely the case. It is possible they read even more than they did thirty or fifty years ago, but in a different way and from different sources: cellphone messages, the internet and various online sites.

Jaroslav Císař,
Čtenář magazine Editor-in-Chief and Czech book
market analyst over many years

I basically feel satisfied astonishment at the constant hunger for books about towns and the places where readers live. I am pleasantly surprised that this hunger has not abated even now that the free book market has been in existence for several decades. The main interest is in factography – documenting the past and natural science topics. Or guidebooks with a personal touch, the kind that connect the past to the present. One big influence on me is that I assess around 200,000 readers in the Sudetenland, i.e. the region where the German population had to move out after the Second World War and the Czech population moved in.

I'm also very pleased that almost every year pleasant surprises often crop up. High-quality books with a big response: big publishing projects and unique monographs.

The most important thing is ultimately:The notion of books as valuable or precious objects has not weakened at all to my mind. I guess, or rather I hope, that this will also be the future of readers and books in the Czech Republic.

MARTIN FRYČ,
bookshop manager in Liberec

Without being fully aware of it, we live in an age of total prosperity. We do not know whether to first choose going to the cinema for twenty possible films or to fifteen theatre performances, ten different exhibitions or if we'll visit fifty sports events, one out of dozens of trendy cafes or fly off somewhere abroad without all that much expense. What books used to give us can nowadays be experienced for real far more than ever before.

As a book editor and small publisher I see the basic problem to be that the book distributors own the publishers and the bookshops and are basically guided by a desire for profit. Hence they primarily present their own books, which are often of a disposable nature. Every day a huge number of them are published. Upon entering a bookshop, ordinary readers are thus thrown back on their own resources and common sense. They are often manipulated by shallow marketing to which they fall prey. They are not trained for anything, which I consider to be a basic task for the more educated and intellectual sections of the population. The intellectual section of the population, which buys, reads and knows the quality of literature is in the minority. It is the same or a similarly small proportion as at other times, when the reading standard was again negatively affected by other political and social factors.

I am not afraid of digitization. Reading trash literature while standing around with a cup of coffee in apartment block communal spaces has only been superseded by reading lifestyle magazines and tabloid articles online. Here the danger is more to do with the ability to handle the truth and a quantity of information. Printed newspapers will disappear. I think that is almost inevitable and understandable development. But books will always be read. Plenty of them.

KAMILA HLADKÁ,
author, editor and owner
of Dcera sestry publishers

For at least thirty years we have been talking of a crisis in readership, the threat of reading illiteracy, the end of printed books and other catastrophes – and yet I think that we still read a lot and that Czech reading is democratic – it is not just a matter for intellectual or other elites and it is not entirely associated with the level of formal education achieved.

A role is certainly played in all this by the excellently operating (when there is no pandemic) branching network of public libraries. Many people take going to a library for granted as part of everyday life. However, publishers do not see the role of libraries as just positive – yes, they purchase our books, arrange forums and authors' readings and generally support books and literature with all their activities, but then on the other hand, by what percentage would the sale of cars, clothes, gardening tools or anything fall if they could be borrowed free of charge? Perhaps the easy availability of books at libraries is associated with the fact that some people see books as something they have a right to that ought to be free or very cheap. The library tradition is not going to change – which is good – but it might be worth considering more substantial compensation for publishers. We might be inspired, for example, by the Scandinavian countries, where public libraries purchase a considerable amount of the print runs of original prose and poetry.

However, I am writing this text in an extraordinary situation – on 11 April 2020, when the libraries and bookshops are closed and people can only buy books online, as the book market is folding. How will this affect reading? Will people realize how they have missed books in quarantine and how much they need them, and as soon as it is possible will they rush back into the bookshops and libraries? I believe and hope that they will - and I do not even want to admit that another, darker possibility may exist.

MARKÉTA HEJKALOVÁ,
writer, translator and organizer of the book
fair at Havlíčkův Brod

It is still the case that the Czechs are above-average readers. Of course we are also seeing a trend whereby one part of the population is moving away from reading books as a pastime towards digital alternatives (e.g. video and social networks), but we still consider the standard of reading as a whole in this country to be very high. Paper books also continue to be seen as high-quality, valuable artefacts. In the Czech Republic, books are very accessible and the density of the bookshop network is above average, as is the network of public libraries. The future of reading in this country will be decided to a large extent by upbringing – parents who guide their children towards reading are laying very firm foundations for their offspring to become lifelong readers.

VÁCLAV KADLEC,
General Director of Albatros, the largest Czech
publishing house

As a librarian I see the pensioners who were used to reading all their lives dying off, so it is highly necessary to focus on the younger generation. Mobile phones, tablets and computers are for the most part more attractive to youngsters than books, so we try by means of various competitions and events at libraries to explain to children and students that reading is irreplaceable.

The common excuse among the middle generation is that they don't have time to read, but in my view it is a question of priorities. Anybody who wants to read will find the time. Personally I am very unpleasantly surprised that at my local secondary school you only need to have read twenty titles to pass the final exam. I would understand if it was twenty books a year. My librarian colleagues and I are still looking for a way to attract people to the library with lectures, forums and creative workshops, while offering them book loans at the same time.

Ludmila Křivancová,
librarian (Karlovy Vary)

To judge by a survey of the internet, reading is becoming a fashionable pursuit – at least in certain social circles. Books are a topic of discussion, as well as the reason behind book community meetings. Whereas both women and men hold lively debates online, bookworm meetings are more a matter for women.

It seems to me that interest is growing in local authors, while the wave of interest in Nordic detective stories is slowly ebbing, and fantasy is still predominant among young adults, often in the original English, even though they are also discovering Czech fantasy authors. Readers are recommending each other books, and the community of booktubers and book influencers, primarily from the younger generation, is growing stronger all the time With the great number of books that are coming out, it is not easy to choose the really high-quality ones. The media professionals only provide a little space for books, so readers resort to online recommendations.

In recent times I have noticed a great increase in the number of audio-books, surprisingly above all amongst the younger generation. Many people have acquired an e-reader, but only use it as a supplement to books, because the classic book is a book after all!

ALENA MORNŠTAJNOVÁ,
writer and translator

Perhaps it is not the very latest thing, but I have noticed it over the long term and consider it to be one of the basic issues: the division of readers into groups and subgroups of fans of various genres. As the hoary old chestnut has it: poetry is only read by those who write it. Sci-fi and fantasy readers do not go for "serious" fiction, and intellectuals scorn popular genres. There are actually no books that everyone might agree upon – and if they ever do (as in the case of *Harry Potter*) it is only because they have agreed on them abroad and the Czech members of the global nerd community adopt him as their own.

PAVEL MANDYS,
journalist, organizer of Magnesia Litera,
the most prestigious Czech literary award

I think we have to distinguish between those who buy books and those who actively read them. They do not make up just one and the same set of people (though I have no hard data). The two certainly overlap, though not entirely by any means. Those who actively read might primarily be library users, while those who buy books do not necessarily read them. I believe the number of readers has not historically changed too much, but the number of buyers most certainly has. The most visible example of this was during the 1980s, when standing in the "Book Thursday" queue was a kind of social statement that did not necessarily mean the text would subsequently be consumed. In my view at least, Czech reading culture is not substantially different from other Central European cultures. The disadvantage of a small language progressively diminishes when books are read in other languages.

Our great strengths undoubtedly include our long tradition, the numerous living classic authors who are still read, and the lively literary scene that is not just in the upper stratosphere of creativity. Our weakness is most certainly the same as what troubles all reading cultures, i.e. the massive growth in other leisure-time and communication options.

Jiří Padevět,
non-fiction author and Director
of the Academia publishing house

Prejudices that young people do not read, the internet is the undoing of printed books and increasing digitization will destroy book culture have, I believe, been refuted. We know from current research into reading that traditional and digital reading (i.e. reading printed books and internet usage) do not rival each other and that various reading platforms coexist without competing. And even if the trend towards electronic documents is clear and irrefutable, the positive attitude towards printed books among Czech readers is also irrefutable. It has been found that specific positive factors associated with books (such as the sense of their physical presence, their smell and the opportunity to leaf through them) are appreciated even amongst younger readers, providing strong grounds for classical reading (and for those who do not read e-books). Hence the question now arises whether and how reading will be altered by the current pandemic emergency, as due to isolation measures most of the supply has naturally shifted into the digital sphere, and there is more usage of online databases, e-books and digital technology. I believe that this crisis will only bolster our attitude to reading and readership.

IRENA PRAZOVÁ,
librarian, co-author of statistical research
into readership among the young population

The great strength of reading culture in the Czech Republic is that at least among the middle and higher age categories there is still mileage in the National Revival myth that our national identity is based on books, so that reading is very much the right thing to do. At the same time this fact is also the great weakness of our attitude towards literature, as en masse we read historicizing texts that only confirm us in the myth of our own innocence and dove-like nature.

In this respect we are doubtless no different from other nations. However, the culture of Jaroslav Hašek, Franz Kafka, Bohumil Hrabal, Josef Jedlička and Jan Zábrana offers the greater potential, i.e. of seeing literature as an opportunity to confront reality.

The focus of the Czech readership is in the hands of primary and secondary school teachers, but alas it is often in thrall to these myths, i.e. to people for whom literature plays a didactic role rather than an encounter with the "other". Hence to this day instead of exposing children to the effects of single paragraphs or chapters, entire lists of literature are taught at schools. But hope is offered by those who teach literature as an opportunity for fresh encounters.

What Vladimír Holan once said about poetry is still true: If we do not treat it well it will move elsewhere. It has enough space. Children can surprise us.

PETR VIZINA,
journalist and rocker

9

Reading in times of civilizational fatigue
Epilogue

> The enjoyment of kitsch is better, in my eyes,
> then the masochism of a reader who reads out of duty
> or to adjust himself to some vogue of art.[91]
>
> (Isaac Bashevis Singer)

Whereas in the previous sections we have circled around Czech reading culture looking at it from several perspectives and shining various spotlights upon it, in this section let us actually use it as a spotlight and shine it on the current state of reading and readership in general, or at least on how it is shown to be by Western civilization, while setting out this summary on the basis of a "trialogue" between a *cultural pessimist,* a *cultural optimist* and a *critical cultural realist.*

DIGITAL TIMES AND THEIR CHALLENGES
It is the view of sociologist Frank Furedi that "the age of the internet is represented as the empowerment of the status of the reader".[92] Polish sociologist Lucyna Stetkiewicz has a similar approach: "The

---

91   Richard Burgin, *Conversation with Isaac Bashevis Singer* (Garden City: Doubleday and Company, 1985), p. 30.
92   Frank Furedi, *Power of Reading. From Socrates to Twitter* (London - Oxford - New York - New Delhi - Sydney: Bloomsbury, 2015) p. 213.

The eye-tracking method

internet is a powerful ally of the book."[93] In contrast, however, it is the common view that the internet rivals reading. We have also come up against this view in our research: people don't read much because they are online a lot: the internet did not use to exist, so people used to read more: the internet is the bane of concentrated reading.

We believe there is no simple answer. Digital reading should be "surrounded" from several sides, just as we have done with Czech reading culture, with statistical data, in the light of user behaviour and ergonomics. *Statistical data* show a clear correlation between

93 Lucyna Stetkiewicz, *Kulturowi wszystkożercy sięgają po książkę. Czytelnictwo ludyczne jako forma uczestnictwa w kulturze literackiej* (Toruń: Wydawnictwo Naukowe Uniwersytetu Mikołaja Kopernika, 2011), p. 364; See i Judith Elkin – Briony Train – Debie Denham, *Reading and Reader Development. The Pleasure of Reading* (London: Facet Publishing, 2003), particularly pp. 173–174.

reading and internet usage.[94] Here we inevitably come up against the age barrier as well as the education barrier in favour of the young and those who have been to college. [obr 16]

Not even if we investigate *user behaviour* do we acquire a picture in which the new medium is ousting the old, but rather user competences are being redefined: the internet is becoming the dominant medium for brief topical texts (e.g. messages, factual information and dictionary entries) or pragmatic informative texts (instructions and information). E-readers attract greater interest on journeys and holidays, but we prefer to deal with books, articles and any long or focused reading in printed media.

Another perspective is that of *ergonomics*, i.e. real-life testing in which we are not just dependent upon the respondents' statements. The literature on this subject has been almost inexhaustible of late.[95] What are we actually measuring and testing? The movement made by our eyes on the paper page and the computer screen, as well as

---

94 See e.g. Miha Kovač, *Never Mind the Web. Here Comes the Book*, pp. 111–115.
95 Several seminal works that we draw from (selection): Naomi S. Baron. *Words Onscreen. The Fate of Reading in a Digital World* (Oxford – New York: Oxford University Press, 2015); Ferris Jabr, "The Reading Brain in the Digital Age: The Science of Paper versus Screens" (2013); online: https://www .scientificamerican.com/article/the-reading-brain-in-the-digital-age-why-paper -still-beats-screens/ [accessed 2018-10-16]; Ziming Liu, "Reading behaviour in the digital environment: Changes in reading behaviour over the past ten years," *Journal of Documentation* 61 (2005), no. 6, pp. 700–712; online: https://pdfs .semanticscholar.org/2dfd/8e98a271cc7d92bde32d216f254c8800e205.pdf [accessed 2018-10-17]; Anne Mangen – Bente R. Walermo – Kolbjørn Brønnick. "Reading linear texts on paper versus computer screen: Effects on reading comprehension," *International Journal of Educational Research* 58 (2013), pp. 61–68; Caroline Myrberg – Ninna Wiberg. "Screen vs. paper: what is the difference for reading and learning", *Insights* 28 (2015), no. 2, pp. 49–54; online: https://www .researchgate.net/publication/281482281_Screen_vs_paper_What_is_the _difference_for_reading_and_learning [accessed 2019-03-19]; Catherine Sheldrick Ross – Lynne (E. F.) McKechnie – Paulette M. Rothbauer. *Reading Still Matters. What Research Reveals about Reading, Libraries and Community* (Santa Barbara – Denver: Libraries Unlimited, 2018); Lauren M. Singer – Patricia A. Alexander. "Reading on Paper and Digitally: What the Past Decades of Empirical Research Reveal," *Review of Educational Research* 87 (2017), no. 6, pp. 1007-1041;

the way in which we are able to remember information from either of these media. The connection between reading as a cognitive operation and our haptics (touch and fine motor skills) is also involved, as is the extent to which the type of medium is associated with our understanding and memorization of what we read.

A few notes at least: there is no great difference when it comes to understanding a text of up to 500 words (about one screen's worth), but for longer texts understanding substantially improves in the case of printed texts: Reading from a monitor is up to a third slower than reading from a printed page. As the digital sphere expands so nonlinear reading also increases and our concentration decreases. Reading onscreen is associated with much greater stress and fatigue. In the case of printed books we have a much greater sense of localization regarding where (i.e. in which part of the text) we are. The digital environment compels us to read more globally, and our concentration on details is much worse, both in terms of text and meaning. The predominant movement made by our eyes on the computer screen is an F-shape: we start in the classic way as in traditional reading (up and then left to right), then we go quickly down, and at a particular moment we again go to the right, but not so much as at first, and then just downwards and so forth.

Here both *cultural optimists* and *cultural pessimists* come unstuck. The former can be glad that good old traditional reading of printed material has managed to hold its ground even against such a huge challenge as the digital revolution. The latter have good reason to wave their finger in admonition and say that what is going on in the digital sphere is an infection that is most definitely going to catch on and soon take the form of a pandemic, as the digital revolution gradually deprives us of the ability to read in a focused way, i.e. the basic essence of reading. The chief representative of this line of thought

Maryanne Wolf, *Tales for Literacy fot the 21st Century* (Oxford: Oxford University Press, 2016).

is German psychiatrist Manfred Spitzer,[96] who says that these processes are progressively affecting our mental functions, and that there is no going back. In his widely quoted book *The Shallows. What the Internet Is Doing to Our Brains* Nicholas Carr is also of the opinion that the digital sphere has its effects upon our memory – and that it is the "technology of forgetfulness", undermining the foundations of our civilization. A "post-literary mind" is being born.[97]

And what does the *critical cultural realist* have to say? He will not have a problem identifying with the Stavanger declaration, in which around 200 experts in reading from all over Europe (and from various scientific fields) combined their voices over the challenges facing our times. On the basis of 54 metastudies with over 170,000 participants they came to the conclusion that printed media are definitely not being edged out by digital media: "comprehension of long-form informational text is stronger when reading on paper than on screens, particularly when the reader is under time pressure". As for digital media, appropriate strategies need to be built up, as "readers are more likely to be overconfident about their comprehension abilities when reading digitally than when reading print."[98] Hence several recommendations such as: "Teachers and other educators must be made aware that rapid and indiscriminate swaps of print, paper and pencils for digital technologies in primary education are not neutral." Other research into this field – it is concluded in the statement – needs to be dealt with as collaboration between technical experts, humanities specialists and social scientists.

Hence a strategy against an impending threat (i.e. that an old medium is under attack by a new medium) is not appropriate. We would

---

96 See Manfred Spitzer, *Digitale Demenz: Wie wir uns und unsere Kinder um den Verstand bringen* (München: Droemer Verlag, 2012); ibid, *Cyberkrank!* (München: Droemer Verlag, 2015).
97 Nicolas Carr, *The Shallows. What the Internet Is Doing to Our Brains* (New York - London: W. W. Norton, 2010), pp. 193 and 112.
98 "Stavanger Declaration Concerning the Future of Reading" (2019); online: https://ereadcost.eu/wp-content/uploads/2019/01/StavangerDeclaration.pdf [accessed 2020-04-05].

prefer to bet on a strategy of collaboration, a new division of roles or convergence, or even *media ecologies*.[99] There is also a historical reason for this. It has happened several times here that the new threatened the old with annihilation. If we go back against the flow of history this primarily means television, which was expected to completely do away with writing. Before that there was film. In the latter half of the 19th century critical voices were raised against magazines, particularly those which made the reader read in a superficial manner due to the very form of the printed page, i.e. the destruction of text linearity. At the end of the 18th century it was thought that the increase in reading and the associated output satisfying the demand for entertainment were harmful, particularly to women, and the chief culprit for this state of affairs was believed to be the novel. So here we see the same pattern repeating, with only its protagonists differing.

We have to accept that the *book–paper–reading* triad,[100] which we understood for so long to be like the Holy Trinity of reading culture, and which we thought to be here forevermore, has now come unstuck on us, as its individual elements have gained their independence. Reading has increasingly made its home beyond paper and books, which have lost their role as the primary medium.

GLUT

In statistical representative research carried out in 2013 we also made enquiries of those who had not bought a single book over the previous year in an effort to discover their reasons. Quite unsurprisingly, the primary reason was book prices. However, we were also

99   Matthew Fuller, *Media Ecologies: Materialist Energies in Art and Technoculture* (Cambridge, MA: MIT Press, 2005); See i Andrew Piper, *Book Was There. Reading in Electronic Times* (Chicago – London: The University of Chicago Press, 2013 [2012]).
100   See Christian Vanderdorpe, *From Papayrus to Hypertext. Towards Universal Digital Library*, transl. by Phylliss Aronoff and Howard Scott (Urbana: University of Illinois Press, 2009 [1999]).

surprised by the ratio of those who did not buy books because there weren't enough on the market to those who did not buy them because there were too many. This ratio was almost 1 to 7, which gave us empirical evidence that Czech reading culture is a saturated culture. It is not so long ago (in the 1980s) that it was a starved culture, when long queues for books stood outside the bookshops: books passed from hand to hand, they were read overnight and the prohibited ones were transcribed on typewriters. Booksellers enjoyed high social prestige, because they were able to oblige their customers with plenty of counter-services – doctors offered them preferential specialist treatment, butchers the best cuts of runp steak, greengrocers hard-to-find foreign fruit like bananas or oranges and actors theatre performance tickets.

All this has ceased to apply to Czech society, not without some regret in many quarters. Czech reading culture has quickly fallen into step with its global counterpart, so that books have entered into a process of rapid *commodification*. However, books by their very nature resist this designation, as the Mexican poet and essayist Gabriel Zaid has said: "We want books to be read by everyone, to be everywhere accessible, but we also want them to continue to be sacred."[101]

The question is how to determine the point where cultural saturation ends and overproduction begins. Besides, the entire history of reading might be dismissed as just a litany of complaints that too many books are coming out, that people are overwhelmed by them and that the important things are being lost in all the mayhem. We might begin with the Old Testament (and the Book of *Ecclesiastes* in particular): "of making many books there is no end; and much study is a weariness of the flesh." (*Ecclesiastes* 12:12). An avalanche of lamentation was unleashed by the invention of printing, since this

---

101   Gabriel Zaid, *So Many Books. Reading and Publishing in an Age of Abundance*, transl. by Natascha Wimmer (Philadelphia: Paul Dry Books, 2003), p. 52.

"Genuinely exhilarating."
—*Leon Wieseltier*

SO
MANY
BOOKS

*Reading and Publishing
in an Age of Abundance*

Gabriel Zaid

Cover of the English
edition of Gabriel Zaid's
Los demasiados libros
(2003)

"Trojan horse of the Germans", as Gutenberg's invention in 1470 was described by Paris professor Guillaume Fichet, was supposedly going to destroy traditional culture, particularly because it would thrust our civilization into an age of endless overproduction. Martin Luther, who disseminated his doctrine thanks to printing, was of the opinion that not so many books should be published, particularly those not dealing with theology. It was at about the same time that Anton Francesco Doni, an Italian social utopian, stated that "there are so many books that we do not even have the time to read their titles". The second half of the 18th century saw a torrent of jeremiads, revelled in by such authors as Johann Wolfgang Goethe and Samuel Taylor Coleridge, as well as various reformist pedagogues: the true art of reading is being lost, and we are overwhelmed by ballast. Reading books is becoming a mere pastime that is far removed from any intellectual claims. Reading lots of books, according to German satirist Georg Christoph Lichtenberg – drags us down into erudite barbarity (*gelehrte Barbarei*). Just as the number of universities has increased over the past 30 to 40-odd years, so their publication output has also radically increased: the "publish or perish" slogan is quite well-known, but this phenomenon is also the target of much criticism: academic ballast is on the rise, and reading is no longer of any importance while publishing is. Despite the total lack of interest among the reading public, books are brought out merely as texts to advance academic careers.[102] The latest great wave of jeremiads targets the internet: we are drowning in the sheer quantity, we are no longer differentiating between what is important and what is not, and our ability to focus our reading is declining (see above).[103]

Let us also have a look at the following figures: around 1950 some 250,000 books saw the light of day worldwide. Twenty years later it was double this figure, and thirty years after that it was double again. In an even broader historical perspective, between 1450 and 1910 some 10 million books are estimated to have been published, while between 1911 and 2009 it was almost 17 times as many (168 million).[104] And because reading (books) is just one of the media activities, the enormous increase in television and radio channels, facilitated by the

---

102   See e.g. Robert Darnton, *Case for Books. Past, Present, and Future* (New York: Public Affairs, 2009), pp. 72-73; Jonathan Rose, Altick's Map: The New Historiography of the Common Reader." In Rosalind Crone – Shafquat Towheed (eds.), *The History od Reading. Volume 3: Methods, Strategies, Tactics* (Basinstoke: Palgrave MacMillan, 2011), p. 23.
103   See also Ilkka Mäkinen, "Reading Like Monks: The Death or Survival of the Love of Reading." In Marju Lauristin – Peeter Vihalemm (eds.), *Reading in Changing Society* (Tartu: University of Tartu Press, 2014), particularly pp. 24-26.
104   See Miha Kovač – Rüdiger Wischenbart, "Globalizationd and publishing." In Angus Phillips – Michael Bhaskar (eds.), *The Oxford Handbook of Publishing* (Oxford – New York: Oxford University Publishing Press, 2019), p. 211.

transition from analog to cable broadcasting, should also be taken into account. Hence not only is our media behaviour changing, but so is our behaviour in general, e.g. "the tendency of ever-available information to blur the boundaries between work and home can affect our personal lives in unexpected ways" (Paul Hemp);[105] so that we are becoming the unwilling slaves of various media, and our time is being fragmentalized into ever shorter and more frequent segments.

Cultural pessimists (catastrophists) will perhaps not be satisfied with historical parallels, objecting that every age lives its own life and that experience from former times is not transferable. Likewise they will also object that what we are living today is not a matter of a higher level of something that used to be here, but an entirely new quality that we have never known before. *Cultural optimists* will say that nothing so revolutionary is going on, i.e. what we are experiencing is just one more in a series, and that we have always been able to cope with all the previous challenges. *Ecclesiastes* has it all, including a solution: "There is nothing new under the sun." (*Ecclesiastes* 1:10). And what about the *critical cultural realist*? He will take all the historical parallels seriously, and will likewise not turn a blind eye to the argument that the amount (or quantity) might now be turning into a new quality, while adding that so far we have not been chronologically detached enough to be able to venture a statement on that. In any case these changes need to be faced, particularly so that we can try to understand them and seek the key to them, as the historical key is an important key, but perhaps not the only one. He might come to the conclusion that at present we have more answers than "right" questions, or we have the information (data, statistics etc.), but we are unable to get to grips with it, because we do not know how to ask the right questions.

---

105   Paul Hemp, "Death by Information Overload," *Harvard Business Review* (September 2009 Issue); online: https://hbr.org/2009/09/death-by-information -overload [accessed 2020-04-06].

READING AND ITS SOCIO-CULTURAL MISSION

Reading (and more generally literacy) is the greatest modernizing force. It entirely transformed western civilization from the mid-18th century to the mid-19th century, turning from a cultural perk for the privileged into a necessity for civilized life. Behind this (inter alia) technological progress we can identify the reason why Western civilization at this time played such a dominant role. It is estimated that between the mid-18th century and the mid-19th century, the number of those in Europe who knew how to read increased tenfold, which can be seen to stem not only from the introduction of compulsory school attendance, but also from the huge demographic growth. The mentality was being entirely transformed,[106] with the huge surge in literacy being partly the cause and partly the consequence. An ever-increasing amount of our knowledge is being mediated by text, which requires the growth of literacy, because as literacy increases so an ever greater proportion of knowledge can be mediated by text. Again it is time for a brief historical excursion.

The first great *mission* associated with reading might be called *enlightenment* (in the broad sense). It used to be believed that literacy in itself made people freer and therefore more open to rational cognition. Thomas Jefferson, the third American President and an author of the *Declaration of Independence* was convinced that literacy of itself was a transforming and liberating force directly leading to aware citizenship. Reading was the primary weapon in the fight against obscurantism. Right from the outset this image was spoilt a little by the reading mania (*Lesewut*) that was raging, particularly in Germany, as its associated symptoms were manifested in the

---

106   See e.g. Guglielmo Cavallo – Roger Chartier (eds.), *A History of Reading in the West*, pp. 284-312; Frank Furedi, *Power of Reading*, pp. s. 91-102; Erich Schön: *Der Verlust der Sinnlichkeit oder Die Verwandlungen des Lesers*; Peter Stein, *Schriftkultur. Eine Geschichte des Schreibens und Lesens* (Darmstadt: WBG, 2006), pp. 253-229.

capitulation to entertaining and escapist reading, which was anything but a source of rational knowledge. The Enlightenment men were rather surprised, if not scared, by this phenomenon, but in any case it was seen as an infantile disorder that civilization just had to get over on its unstoppable way towards progress. One accompanying feature of this enlightenment mission was faith in such institutes of learning as schools, various associations and reading clubs. It was believed that what was neglected in the family could be made up for with the help of these establishments. At first this mission had tasks that were civilizing and ultimately democratizing. The former included the expansion of literacy and education, the latter the lowering of book availability thresholds, meaning primarily their price, so that those who could not afford to own them might at least borrow them. The paradox behind the enlightenment mission is that apart from this universal task it also facilitated the emergence of linguistic-ethnic nationalisms (national movements), because as the sphere of the word expanded, it gave rise to a need for texts addressing ever broader strata of the reading community, who wanted to read in their native languages.

Next in line is the *bourgeois mission*. As literacy increased so the urban population increasingly started to come to the fore. Reading (and more broadly culture) can be said to have become a secular religion and a programme for personal growth and cultural emancipation. Increasingly reading started to move into towns everywhere. As German cultural historian Jost Schneider commented: "Literacy follows industrialization, and democratization follows literacy."[107] The extent of urbanization everywhere is thus also the extent of literacy.[108] The bourgeois cultural model will no longer be satisfied with the mere mastery of reading as a civilized skill. A more challenging

---

107   Jost Schneider, *Sozialgeschichte des Lesens*, p. 272
108   See e.g. Jeffrey Brooks, *When Russia Learned to Read. Literacy and Popular Literature 1861-1917* (Evanston: Northwestern University Press, 2003 [1985]), pp. 12-14.

programme needs to be established, higher tasks need to be set, and new space needs to be provided for cultural identification for those who want more. This way the advent of modernism in the latter half of the 19th century might also be explained. This introduces tension between the independent artist and the dejected urbanite, i.e. between cultural-symbolic capital and economic-social capital.[109] At the same time it is paradoxically none other than the urbanites who have looked after the artist and his social emancipation ever since the Enlightenment. However, what the artist is now demanding is aesthetic emancipation.

It only remains to be asked where readers of modernist works may be found. We find them primarily among editors, journalists and academics. They are not a commonly found group, but highly vocal. Specifically, to quote Jonathan Rose, they engage in "coterie readership"[110] which is supposed to be a kind of higher initiation, an initiation into an elite culture, a culture of higher demands and ambitions. A spirit of snobbery and aesthetic privilege hovers over these circles. Reproaches of a certain hermeticism and "sterile obscurantism" (Roger Dataller)[111] are deflected by supporters of modernism by saying that this art is not meant for the masses, or at least not for the masses of the times in question, and that it is preparing the path into the future.

We might call the subsequent mission the *broad horizons mission*, or the multimedia mission, where two processes combine: the emancipating potential of reading appears to be exhausted and at the same time we need to enter the stage of "negotiating" with other media. The golden age of books (and the printed word in general) ends around the First World War and the new mass media (film, radio and television) gradually start to emerge. One important factor in all this

---

109 See Pierre Bourdieu, *The Rules of Arts. Genesis and Structure of the Literary Field*, transl. by Susan Emanuel (Stanford: Stanford University Press 1996 [1992]).
110 Jonathan Rose, *The Intellectual Life of the British Working Classes*, p. 426.
111 Cited from Jonathan Rose, *The Intellectual Life of the British Working Classes*, p. 426.

is that reading comes to be just one of several activities in a multimedia society, while television in particular is seen as its greatest rival in the West. Hence a great dilemma arises: to be a culturally higher alternative to television, i.e. an activity for a select elite, or to enter into combat with mass media, thus *de facto* recalling that the book was actually the first mass-distributed object after the invention of printing.[112]

In any case here a certain disparity opens up. Since the 1970s this state has sometimes been seen as culturally damaging, while the cultural *niveau* itself has started developing towards an increasing acceptance of the "lowbrow", albeit more in America than in Europe. Those who were committed to the "highbrow" repertoire, are now increasingly willing to read the "lowbrow". However, this does not apply the other way round. In other words, a university professor is increasingly more likely to read a detective novel, which a generation or two earlier he might have considered to be a waste of time and a profanation of his sociocultural status, than a supermarket assistant is likely to read Virginia Woolf or James Joyce. This is not just a printed-word cultural phenomenon, but something that (perhaps even more so) also affects music, theatre and visual art. It might be described as fatigue brought about by modernist experiments. They are what have caused the world of literature and the world of reading to separate.[113] Basic reading behaviour has expanded considerably with regard to repertoire and functions. The bourgeois reading model encompassing individual growth and cultural emancipation has dissolved into an "omnivorousness" reading model.[114]

---

112   See e.g. John Sutherland. *Bestsellers. A Very Short Introduction* (Oxford: Oxford University Press, 2007), p. 23.
113   See e.g. Molly Abel Travis, *Reading Cultures. The Construction of Readers in the Twentieth Century* (Carbondale - Edwardsville: Southern Illinois University Press, 1998), pp. 18-43.
114   See e.g. Lucyna Stetkiewicz, *Kulturowi wszystkożercy sięgają po książkę*, particularly p. 93; Richard A. Peterson - Roger M. Kern, "Changing highbrow taste: from snob to omnivore," *American Sociological Review* 61 (1996), no. 5, pp. 900-907.

MISSION FOR OUR TIMES SOUGHT

So here we are in the digital revolution. We shall leave the question open whether this involves a new quality or is simply an expansion of the field. For *cultural pessimists* this means that reading has already exhausted its civilizing programme and no other is on the horizon, i.e. there is no mission that can be compared to the previous one. Reading managed to cope with civilizational difficulties, but it has been rather caught unawares by problems over levels. *Cultural optimists* will say that nothing much is the matter, as reading is not a sub--competence but a key competence that other media competences develop. They will have sufficient arguments for this from various research, while they will also add that the state of western society does not apply to the world as a whole. In sub-Saharan Africa, majority illiteracy is still predominant. In many other poor countries, reading comes up against the problem of the availability of books and reading material in general. *Critical cultural realists* will take the argument seriously about the civilizational exhaustion of the project called reading, but at the same time they will not forget to ask whether some new mission is in the air.

It might be the mission which ascribes the role of a key competence to reading in the fight against disinformation or *fake news*.[115] This involves a strong period factor that stems in particular from the huge increase in information and its easy availability. Although reading is nowadays just one of the media competences, it is still the most crucial, i.e. the one that equips us for other media activities. At the same time this should not be just limited to expert circles (particularly academic ones), but a competence that reaches into the broadest possible circles.[116]

---

115 See e.g. National Literacy Trust, *Fake News and Critical Literacy* (2016); online: https://literacytrust.org.uk/research-services/research-reports/fake-news -and-critical-literacy-final-report/ [accessed 2019-02-12].

116 See e.g. Magnus Persson, "The Hidden Foundation of Critical Reading." In Paulette M. Rothbauer – Kjell Ivar Skjerdingstad – Lynne (E. F.) McKechnie – Knut Oterholm (eds.), *Plotting the Reading Experience. Theory, Practice, Politics*

The famous American neuropsychologist Maryanne Wolf sees the opportunity for a new mission in reading going back to its roots – to deep reading, the performance of which involves slow, focused reading; as the only way for us to become complete. Only that way do we manage to transform the gathered information into knowledge, and that knowledge into wisdom.[117] From this perspective, reading is not just the technical collection of information, but it is much more a specific decision, namely a decision on the kind of attitude and perceptivity required. To quote Alan Jacobs, to whom Maryanne Wolf refers, this involves "a particular form of attention" and "blessed moments".[118]

Another attempt (the third) at formulating the new mission gives us *ludic reading*. That is what Polish sociologist Lucyna Stetkewicz,[119] supported to a large extent by her own research, calls the way in which a positive attitude ought to be fostered, particularly among young people. They should not be bullied with large amounts of compulsory reading, and the "highbrow" (elite) and "lowbrow" (popular) literature dichotomy should be abandoned, along with the pedagogical fear of popular literature. Deep-rooted prejudices should not be insisted upon and more contact should be established with the actual (empirical) reader and his or her real needs. Something of a return to our childhood perception of the world is involved here, i.e. to a way that leaves no room for boredom even if it is disguised by high cultural prestige. This way of looking at things does not allow for anything like "a good book but a boring one". Either it is boring or it is good.[120]

And there is one more mission, whose name is *family* – i.e. the primary socializing environment and at the same time the primary

(Waterloo: Wilfried Laurier University Press, 2016), pp. 19-36.
117 Maryanne Wolf, *Reader, Come Home. The Reading Brain in a Digital World* (New York: Harper Collins Publishers, 2018).
118 Alan Jacobs, *The Pleasures of Reading in an Age of Distraction* (Oxford - New York: Oxford University Press, 2011), pp. 149-150.
119 Lucyna Stetkiewicz, *Kulturowi wszystkożercy sięgają po książkę*.
120 See Grzegorz Leszczyński, *Wielkie małe książki. Lektury dzieci. I nie tylko* (Poznań: Media Rodzina, 2015), particularly pp. 120-121.

culture-creating matrix. This is of decisive importance mainly because it is the initial one. There will be no other "for the first time" in our lives including our cultural reading lives. What is neglected here will create obstacles later. Hence it is highly likely that the child who does not come across reading until school is going to associate it with something unpleasant. On the other hand, however, your family is not your destiny (or predestination), as its shortcomings, including the cultural ones, can be made up for in future life, but never replaced and never at all taken over, as "society cannot assume the individual functions of the family without at the same time weakening it." That is the judgement of Vladislav Chvála and Ludmila Trapková, a Czech psychotherapist and Czech psychologist, both with many years of experience as family therapists.[121]

In other words, in all four cases we are coming back somewhere. If we want to find out where then in the first instance it would be enlightenment criticism. In the second case it is a return to the contemplative reading of the monastic orders in the Middle Ages (as an antidote to our hurried digital age), while this return is also mirrored in all the "slow" movements, such as slow food and slow travelling. In the third case we again see the Epicureanism of classical antiquity and its latter-day echoes in various *pleasures of reading* style activities. And the fourth case? Here we come back to that same primary social and cultural matrix. If we want to give it a name then let us call it Freudian inspiration, as it was Sigmund Freud who said that the primary complex of relations, values and dependencies stems from the family, and that a person is formed in the first six years of life. Everything that comes afterwards is just a repetition of the initial setting.

The critical cultural realists will ultimately not forget to ask if these four attempts have the potential to be those truly great missions, i.e. just like the previous missions. As a by-product of this question, they

121   Ludmila Trapková - Vladislav Chvála, "Rodina jako organismus." In Václav Cílek - Alexander Ač and others, *Věk nerovnováhy. Klimatická změna, bezpečnost a cesty k národní resilienci* (Praha: Academia, 2019), p. 227.

are compelled to realize that those much-desired great missions need to be sought more in retrospect, i.e. in reflections of the past and re-evaluations of past models.

Ultimately this is not a pessimistic finding at all, as we arrive at the following square:

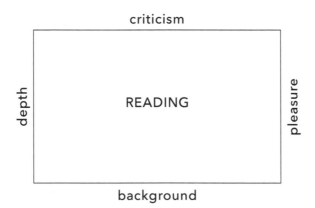

criticism – fighting *fake news*, building up resistance in the face of the *attention economy* and thus also disrupting the *disinformation ecosystem*;

pleasure – blurring the boundaries between "highbrow" and "lowbrow", destigmatizing genre literature, returning to reading as entertainment (in the broadest sense);

depth – *deep reading*, slowness, thoroughness, developing a sense for the linear quality of a text;

background – the family as the first *socializing environment*, its irreplaceability in reader socialization, the awareness that this is an environment for beginnings and that there will be no other initial environment.

This is an area that might be called the square of constantly sustainable readership in a version for the early 21st century, which may well be a time of civilizational fatigue, but it is definitely not entirely barren.

SUMMARY AND CONCLUSIONS

Reading has come to be taken for granted amongst those of us in Western cultures. Its civilizing potential now seems to be exhausted. Basically it no longer has anywhere to grow. We have all learnt to read. The problem is no longer just the availability of what we want to read. Quite the reverse. We are drowning in the surplus. In the digital age the distance between us and our reading material has been slashed. Moreover, in liberal democracies nothing is prohibited (apart from clearly defined legal cases such as racial intolerance), so that the tension between the individual and the establishment is disappearing. There is a lack of an adversary. Reading used to be able to cope with overcoming civilizational obstacles, but the question is now how to cope with difficulties of "levels". We read because we read... nothing more. It is all part of our basic civilizational equipment full stop. There is no other "social order", except in the developing world, where what we take for granted in the West is still an unattainable dream. Reading has become an exhausted project or rather the project of a civilizationally fatigued time. Hence the road forwards very often leads backwards – to a re-evaluation of previous ways and a search for lost ways.

And yet reading has become something we take for granted, and turns out again and again that it is a "cultural project" that we have to handle, work with or at least sustain. This means that again and again we have to adapt it to the needs of each new age, because "we are never born to read," as Maryanne Wolf says,[122] and "Readers are made, not born. No one comes into the world already predisposed for and against print." (Aidan Chambers).[123]

---

122 Maryanne Wolf, *Proust and the Squid. The Story and Science of the Reading Brain* (London: Icon Books, 2008 [2007]), p. 3.
123 Aidan Chambers, *The Reading Environment. How Adults Help Children Enjoy Books* (Stroud: Thimble Press, 1973), p. 16.

Bibliography

ALTER, Robert. *The Pleasures of Reading in an Ideological Age* (New York – London: W. W. Norton 1996 [1989]).

"Babička po 150 letech děti už nezajímá," *iDNES* (29. 12. 2004); online: https://www.idnes.cz/kultura/literatura/babicka-po-150-letech-deti-uz-nezajima.A041229_113156_literatura_gra [accessed 2020-04-03].

BAJAJA, Antonín. "Chybí mi tu dobří čtenáři," interview by Ondřej Nezbeda, *Respekt* 21 (2010), no. 12, pp. 38–41.

BARON, Naomi S. *Words Onscreen. The Fate of Reading in a Digital World* (Oxford – New York: Oxford University Press, 2015).

BARONOVÁ, Barbora. "Knižní trh se zhroutil jako domino," interview by Petr Vizina (podcast, 8. 4. 2020); online: https://magazin.aktualne.cz/kultura/literatura/pocast-petra-viziny-knizni-trh-se-zhroutil-jako-domino-rika/r~eadd9b7879id11ea9d470cc47ab5f122/ [accessed 2020-04-08].

BARTHES, Roland. *The Pleasure of the Text*, transl. by Robert Miller (New York: Hill and Wang, 1975 [1973]).

BAUMGÄRTNER, Alfred Clemens (ed.). *Lesen. Ein Handbuch* (Hamburg: Verlag für Buchmarkt-Forschung, 1974).

BAUMAN, Zygmunt. *Liquid Modernity* (Cambridge: Polity Press, 2000).

BECKER, Paula. *Looking for Betty MacDonald. The Egg, the Plague, Mrs. Piggle-Wiggle, and I* (Washington: University of Washington Press, 2016).

BOHN, Roger E. – SHORT, James E. *How Much Information? Report on American Consumers* (San Diego: Global Information Industry Center – University of California, 2009); online: https://group47.com/HMI_2009_ConsumerReport_Dec9_2009.pdf [accessed 2020-04-05]

BOHNSACK, Petra – FOLTIN, Hans-Friedrich (eds.). *Lesekultur. Populäre Lesestoffe von Gutenberg bis zum Internet* (Marburg: Universitätsbibliothek, 1999).

BOURDIEU, Pierre. *The Rules of Arts. Genesis and Structure of the Literary Field*, transl. by Susan Emanuel (Stanford: Stanford University Press 1996 [1992]).

BRIGGS, Asa – BURKE, Peter. *A Social History of the Media. From Gutenberg io the Internet* (Cambridge: Polity Press, 2005).

BROOKS, Jeffrey. *When Russia Learned to Read. Literacy and Popular Literature 1861–1917* (Evanston: Northwestern University Press, 2003 [1985]).

BURGIN, Richard. *Conversation with Isaac Bashevis Singer* (Garden City: Doubleday and Company, 1985).

BURKE, Peter. *Languages and Communication in Early Modern Europe* (Cambridge: Cambridge University Press, 2004).

BRZOBOHATÝ, Martin. *Čtenářství a Facebook* (Brno: FF MU, 2017); online: https://is.muni.cz/th/spdkw/VerzeTisk.pdf [accessed 2020-04-03].

CARR, Nicolas. *The Shallows. What the Internet Is Doing to Our Brains* (New York – London: W. W. Norton, 2010).

CAVALLO, Guglielmo – CHARTIER, Roger (eds.). *A History of Reading in the West*, transl. by Lydia G. Cochrane (Amherst – Boston: University of Massachusetts Press, 2003 [1997]).

CHAMBERS, Aidan. *The Reading Environment. How Adults Help Children Enjoy Books* (Stround: Thimble Press, 1973).

CHARTIER, Roger. *The Order of Books*, transl. by Lydia G. Cochrane (Stanford: Stanford University Press, 1994 [1992]).

CHYMKOWSKI, Roman. *Autobiografie lekturowe studentów* (Warszawa: Biblioteka Narodowa, 2011).

CIHELKOVÁ, Barbora. "Zrušte Babičku, nerozumíme jí," *Lidové noviny* 13. 10. 2015, p. 14.

CÍLEK, Václav. "Zneklidňující množství knih," interview by Svatava Antošová, *Tvar* 22 (2011), no. 3, p. 1 and 4–5.

DARNTON, Robert. *Case for Books. Past, Present, and Future* (New York: Public Affairs, 2009).

DE MAN, Paul. *Allegories of Reading. Figural Language in Rousseau, Nietzsche, Rilke, and Proust* (New Haven – London: Yale University Press, 1979).

DUNIN, Janusz. *Pismo zmienia świat. Czytanie, lektura, czytelnictwo* (Warszawa: Wydawnictwo Naukowe, 1998).

Dvořák, Stanislav. "Boj o chobotnici na Letné," *Novinky* (26. 10. 2007); online: https://www.novinky.cz/specialy/clanek/tema-boj-o-chobotnici-na-letne-39630 [accessed 2020-04-03].

Dymmel, Anna. "Kultura czytelnicza – teoria i praktika." In Dymmel, Anna – Kotuła, Sebastian Dawid – Znajomski, Artur (eds.), *Kultura czytelnicza i informacyjna – teoria i praktyka. Wybrane zagadnienia* (Lublin: Wydawnictwo Uniwersytetu Marii Curii-Skłodowskiej, 2015).

Eggert, Hartmut – Garbe, Christine. *Literarische Sozialisation* (Stuttgart: J. B. Metzler, 2003).

Elkin, Judith – Train, Briony – Denham, Debie. *Reading and Reader Development. The Pleasure of Reading* (London: Facet Publishing, 2003).

Engelsing, Rolf. "Die Perioden der Lesergeschichte in der Neuzeit: Das statistische Ausmass und die soziokulturelle Bedeutung der Lektüre," *Archiv für Geschichte des Buchwesens* 10 (1970), pp. 944–1002.

———. *Der Bürger als Leser. Lesergeschichte in Deutschland* (Stuttgart: J. B. Metzler, 1973).

Farrell, Grace (ed.). *Isaac Bashevis Singer. Conversations* (Jackson – London: University Press of Mississippi, 1992).

Fibiger, Martin. *Vztah gymnazistů a vysokoškoláků ke knize, čtení a literární výchově* (Ústí nad Labem: Univerzita J. E. Purkyně, 2013).

Frey, Jaroslav. "Práce se čtenářem," *Knihovna* 3 (1948), pp. 91–95.

Fuller, Matthew. *Media Ecologies: Materialist Energies in Art and Technoculture* (Cambridge, MA: MIT Press, 2005).

Furedi, Frank. *Power of Reading. From Socrates to Twitter* (London – Oxford – New York – New Delhi –Sydney: Bloomsbury, 2015).

Gold, Joseph. *Read For Your Life. Literature as a Life Support System* (Allston: Fitzhenry & Whiteside 2001 [1990]).

Halada, Jan. *Encyklopedie českých nakladatelství 1949–2006* (Praha: Libri, 2007).

Haman, Aleš. *Literatura z pohledu čtenářů* (Praha: Československý spisovatel, 1991).

Heger, Juraj. "Knihy levnější být nemůžou," interview by Petra Tesařová, *Lidové noviny* 22. 3. 2011, p. 14.

Hemp, Paul. "Death by Information Overload," *Harvard Business Review* (September 2009 Issue); online: https://hbr.org/2009/09/death-by-information-overload [accessed 2020-04-06].

HEJKALOVÁ, Markéta. "Malí a velcí srdcaři", *H7O* (2. 4. 2020); online: http://www.h7o.cz/den/ctvrtek/ [accessed 2020-04-02].

HROCH, Miroslav. *Na prahu národní existence. Touha a skutečnost* (Praha: Mladá fronta, 1999).

JABR, Ferris. "The Reading Brain in the Digital Age: The Science of Paper versus Screens" (2013); online: https://www.scientificamerican.com/article/the-reading-brain-in-the-digital-age-why-paper-still-beats-screens/ [accessed 2018-10-16].

JACOBS, Alan. *The Pleasures of Reading in an Age of Distraction* (Oxford – New York: Oxford University Press, 2011).

JENKINS, Henry. *Convergence Culture. Where Old and New Media Collide* (New York – London: New York University Press, 2006).

JOHNSON, William A. *Readers and Reading Culture in the High Roman Empire* (Oxford: Oxford University Press, 2010).

"Klaus: Chobotnici na Letné zabráním i vlastním tělem," *iDNES* (3. 5. 2007); online: https://www.idnes.cz/zpravy/domaci/klaus-chobotnici-na-letne-zabranim-i-vlastnim-telem.A070503_160531_domaci_pei [accessed 2020-04-03].

KONRÁD, Daniel. "Zaorálek hodil knižní trh přes palubu, tvrdí knihkupci. Luxor bez pomoci neotevře," (9. 4. 2020); online: https://magazin.aktualne.cz/kultura/literatura/zaoralek-hodil-knizni-trh-pres-palubu-knihkupectvi-luxor/r~cad156fe7a6111ea8b230cc47ab5f122/ [accessed 2020-04-09].

KORYŚ, Izabela – CHYMKOWSKI, Roman – ZASACKA, Sofia. *Stan czytelnictwa w Polsce w 2017 roku* (Warzsawa: Biblioteka Narodowa, 2018); online: https://www.bn.org.pl/download/document/1529572435.pdf [accessed 2020-04-07].

KOVAČ, Miha. *Never Mind the Web. Here Comes the Book* (Oxford: Chandos Publishing, 2008).

KOVAČ, Miha – WISCHEBART, Rüdiger. "Globalizationd and publishing." In Phillips, Angus – Bhaskar, Michael (eds.), *The Oxford Handbook of Publishing* (Oxford – New York: Oxford University Publishing Press, 2019), pp. 207–225.

KURSCHUS, Stephanie. *European Book Cultures. Diversity as a Challenge* (Wiesbaden: Springer VS, 2015).

LESŇÁK, Rudolf. *Horizonty čitateľskej kultúry* (Bratislava: Slovenský spisovateľ, 1991).

"Lesesozialisation in der Familie" (2009); online: http://www.lesen-in
-deutschland.de/html/content.php?object=journal&lid=923 [accessed
2020-04-04].

LESZCZYŃSKI, Grzegorz. *Wielkie małe książki. Lektury dzieci. I nie tylko* (Poznań: Media Rodzina, 2015).

LISHAUGEN, Roar. "Incompatible Reading Cultures: Czech Common Readers and
the Soviet Mass Reader Concept of the Early 1950s", *Scando-Slavica* 21 (2014),
no. 1 (60), pp. 108–127.

LIU, Ziming. "Reading behaviour in the digital environment: Changes in reading behaviour over the past ten years," *Journal of Documentation* 61 (2005),
no. 6, pp. 700–712; online: https://pdfs.semanticscholar.org/2dfd/8e98a271c
c7d92bde32d216f254c8800e205.pdf [accessed 2018-10-17].

LUKÁŠ, František. "Úvaha o literatuře tzv. nedostatkové," *Kulturní tvorba* 3 (1965),
no. 8, p. 8.

LYONS, Martyn. *A History of Reading and Writing in the Western World*, London: Palgrave Macmillan, 2010.

———. *Books. A Living History* (London: Thames & Hudson, 2013 [2011]).

MÄKINEN, Ilkka. "Reading Like Monks: The Death or Survival of the Love of Reading." In Lauristin, Marju – Vihalemm, Peeter (eds.). *Reading in Changing Society*
(Tartu: University of Tartu Press, 2014).

MANGEN, Anne – WALERMO Bente R. – BRØNNICK Kolbjørn. "Reading linear texts
on paper versus computer screen: Effects on reading comprehension," *International Journal of Educational Research* 58 (2013), pp. 61–68.

MUSILOVÁ, Anna. "Knižní influencerka: Češi jsou čtenáři. Cpát dětem Babičku je
fatální chyba" (23. 8. 2017); online: https://www.idnes.cz/zpravy/lide-ceska
/lucie-zelinkova-knizni-influencerka-rozhovor-lide- ceska.A170814_144631
_lide-ceska_amu [accessed 2020-04-03].

MYRBERG, Caroline – WIBERG, Ninna. "Screen vs. paper: what is the difference
for reading and learning", *Insights* 28 (2015), no. 2, pp. 49–54; online: https://
www.researchgate.net/publication/281482281_Screen_vs_paper_What_is
_the_difference_for_reading_and_learning [accessed 2019-03-19].

"Nahradí Babičku Harry Potter?", *iDNES* (17. 7. 2015); online: https://www.idnes
.cz/zpravy/domaci/povinna-cetba-ve-skole.A150715_205812_domaci_zt
[accessed 2020-04-03].

Nápravník, Milan. "O sounáležitosti surrealisty," interview by Irena Zítková, *Nové knihy* 33 (1994), no. 9, p. 9.

National Endowment for the Arts, *To Read or Not To Read. A Question of National Consequence* (2007); online: https://www.arts.gov/sites/default/files/ToRead .pdf [accessed 2020-04-07].

National Literacy Trust. *Fake News and Critical Literacy* (2016); online: https:// literacytrust.org.uk/research-services/research-reports/fake-news-and-critical -literacy-final-report/ [accessed 2019-02-12].

Pavlik, Devana. "The History of the Book in the Czech Republic and Slovakia," In Suarez, Michael F. –Woudhuysen, H. R. (eds.), *The Book. A Global History* (Oxford: Oxford University Press, 2013), pp. 461–469.

Persson, Magnus. "The Hidden Foundation of Critical Reading." In Rothbauer, Paulette M. – Skjerdingstad, Kjell Ivar – McKechnie, Lynne (E.F.) – Oterholm, Knut (eds.), *Plotting the Reading Experience. Theory, Practice, Politics* (Waterloo: Wilfried Laurier University Press, 2016), pp. 19–36.

Peterson, Richard A. – Kern, Roger M. "Changing highbrow taste: from snob to omnivore," *American Sociological Review* 61 (1996), no. 5, pp. 900–907.

Phillips, Angus – Bhaskar, Michael (eds.). *The Oxford Handbook of Publishing* (Oxford – New York: Oxford University Publishing Press, 2019).

Piper, Andrew. *Book Was There. Reading in Electronic Times* (Chicago – London: The University of Chicago Press, 2013 [2012]).

Přibáň, Michal and co. *Český literární samizdat 1949–1989. Edice, časopisy, sborníky* (Praha: Academia – Institute of Czech Literature, CAS, 2018).

Riesz, János – Schmidt-Hannisa, Hans-Walter (eds.). *Lesekulturen. Reading Cultures* (Frankfurt am Main: Peter Lang, 2003).

Richter, Vít. "Benchmarking knihoven a německý Bibliothekindex." In Šedá, Marie (ed.). *Knihovna pro všechny* (Ostrava: Moravskoslezská vědecká knihovna, 2015), pp. 6–24; online: https://katalog.svkos.cz/exlibris/aleph /a22_1/apache_media/337UYS77J2KQXBFLLA9EVR2YEIN667.pdf [accessed 2020-04-06].

Richter, Vít – Pillerová, Vladana. *Analýza věkové, vzdělanostní a mzdové struktury pracovníků knihoven ČR 2016/2017. Zpráva z průzkumu* (Praha: Národní knihovna, 2017); online: https://www.vkol.cz/uploads/page/171/doc /analyza-vzdelavani-zprava-2017-def.pdf [accessed 2020-04-02].

Rose, Jonathan. "The History of Education as the History of Reading," *History of Education* 3 (2007), nos. 4–5, pp. 595–605; online: https://www.tandfonline.com/doi/abs/10.1080/00467600701496922?journalCode=thed20 [accessed 2020-04-01].

——. *The Intelectual Life of the British Working Classes* (New Haven – London: 2010 [2002]).

——. Altick's Map: The New Historiography of the Common Reader." In Crone, Rosalind – Towheed, Shafquat (eds.). *The History od Reading. Volume 3: Methods, Strategies, Tactics* (Basinstoke: Palgrave MacMillan), 2011, pp. 15–26.

Ross, Catherine Sheldrick – McKechnie, Lynne (E. F.) – Rothbauer, Paulette M. *Reading Still Matters. What Research Reveals about Reading, Libraries and Community* (Santa Barbara – Denver: Libraries Unlimited, 2018).

Sabine, Gordon and Patricia. *Books That Made the Difference. What People Told Us* (Hamden: Library of Professional Publications 1984 [1983]).

Schmidtchen, Gerhard. *Lesekultur in Deutschland. Ergebnisse repräsentative Buchmarktstudien für den Börsenverein des Deutschen Buchhandels* (Frankfurt am Main: Börseverein des Deutschen Buchhandels, 1968).

Schneider, Jost. *Sozialgeschichte des Lesens. Zur historischen Entwicklung und sozialen Differenzierung der literarischen Kommunikation in Deutschlad* (Berlin – New York: de Gruyter, 2004).

Schön, Erich. *Der Verlust der Sinnlichkeit oder Die Verwandlungen des Lesers. Mentalitätswandel um 1800* (Stuttgart: Klett-Cotta, 1987).

——. "'Lesekultur' – Einige historische Klärungen." In: Rosebrock, Cornelia, (ed.). *Lesen im Medienzeitalter* (Weinheim – München: Juventa, 1995), pp. 137–164.

Siekierski, Stanisław. *Czytania Polaków w XX wieku* (Warszawa: Wydawnictwo Uniwersytetu Warszawskiego, 2000).

Singer, Lauren M. – Alexander, Patricia A. "Reading on Paper and Digitally: What the Past Decades of Empirical Research Reveal," *Review of Educational Research* 87 (2017), no. 6, pp. 1007–1041.

Skibińska, Małgorzata. "Książka. Symbolika, metaforyka." In Żbikowska-Migoń, Anna – Skalska-Zlat, Marta (eds.), *Encyklopedia książki* (Wrocław: Wydawnictwo Uniwersytetu Wrocławskiego, 2017), pp. 216–221.

SOCHA, Irena. "Lektura – przekaz, komunikacja czy relacja?" In Żbikowska-Migoń, Anna – Skalska Zlat, Marta (eds.), *Encyklopedia książki* (Wrocław: Wydawnictwo Uniwersytetu Wrocławskiego, 2017), pp. 99–113.

SPITZER, Manfred. *Digitale Demenz: Wie wir uns und unsere Kinder um den Verstand bringen* (München: Droemer Verlag, 2012).

———. *Cyberkrank!* (München: Droemer Verlag, 2015).

STANOVICH, Keith E. "Matthew Effect in Reading: Some Consequences of Individual Differences in the Acquisition of Literacy," *Reading Research Quarterly* 21 (Fall 1986), pp. 360–407; online: http://www.keithstanovich.com/Site/Research_on_Reading_files/RRQ86A.pdf [accessed 2020-04-13].

"Stavanger Declaration Concerning the Future of Reading" (2019); online: https://ereadcost.eu/wp-content/uploads/2019/01/StavangerDeclaration.pdf [accessed 2020-04-05].

STEIN, Peter. *Schriftkultur. Eine Geschichte des Schreibens und Lesens* (Darmstadt: WBG, 2006).

STEINBERG, Heinz. "Books and readers as subject of research in Europe and America," *International Social Science Journal* 24 (1972), no. 4, pp. 744–755.

STETKIEWICZ, Lucyna. *Kulturowi wszystkożercy sięgają po książkę. Czytelnictwo ludyczne jako forma uczestnictwa w kulturze literackiej* (Toruń: Wydawnictwo Naukowe Uniwersytetu Mikołaja Kopernika, 2011).

STIFTUNG LESEN. *Lesen in Deutschland 2008* (2008); online: https://www.stiftunglesen.de/download.php?type=documentpdf&id=11 [accessed 2020-04-07].

STØLE, Hildegunn. "Why digital natives need books: The myth of the digital native," *First Monday* 23 (2018), no. 10, non-paged; online: https://journals.uic.edu/ojs/index.php/fm/article/view/9422/7594 [accessed 2019-04-15].

SUTHERLAND, John. *Bestsellers. A Very Short Introduction* (Oxford: Oxford University Press, 2007).

SÝKOROVÁ, Petra. "Když nabídka likviduje poptávku," *Profit* 21 (2010), no. 14, pp. 18–23.

ŠIMEČEK, Zdeněk – TRÁVNÍČEK, Jiří. *Knihy kupovati... Dějiny knižního trhu v českých zemích* (Praha: Academia, 2014).

ŠMEJKALOVÁ, Jiřina. *Cold War Books in the 'Other' Europe And What Came After* (Leiden – Boston: Brill, 2011).

Šrámková, Jana. "Na cestách s paní Dallowayovou," interview by Ondřej Kavalír, *Grand Biblio* 3 (2009), no. II, pp. 4–5.

Thon, Jan. *Osvětou k svobodě. Kniha o českých čtenářích* (Praha: Aventinum, 1948).

Trapková, Ludmila – Chvála, Vladislav. "Rodina jako organismus." In Cílek, Václav – Ač, Alexander and co. *Věk nerovnováhy. Klimatická změna, bezpečnost a cesty k národní resilienci* (Praha: Academia, 2019).

Travis, Molly Abel. *Reading Cultures. The Construction of Readers in the Twentieth Century* (Carbondale – Edwardsville: Southern Illinois University Press, 1998).

Trávníček, Jiří. *Překnížkováno. Co čteme a kupujeme (2013)* (Brno – Praha: Host – Národní knihovna ČR, 2014).

———. *Reading Bohemia. Readers and Reading in the Czech Republic at the Beginning of the 21th Century*, transl. by Melvyn Clarke (Praha: Akropolis – Institute of Czech Literature, CAS, 2015).

———. "Reading and Our Life Stories," *Open Cultural Studies* 2 (2018), pp. 591–597.

———. *Kulturní vetřelec. Dějiny čtení – kalendárium* (Brno: Host, 2020).

Vaculík, Ludvík. *Hodiny klavíru* (Brno: Atlantis, 2007).

Vanderdorpe, Christian. *From Papyrus to Hypertext. Towards Universal Digital Library*, transl. by Phylliss Aronoff and Howard Scott (Urbana: University of Illinois Press, 2009 [1999]).

van der Weel, Andriaan. *Changing Our Textual Minds. Towards a Digital Order of Knowledge* (Manchester – New York: Manchester University Press, 2011).

Wachtel, Andrew. *Remaining Relevant after Communism. The Role of the Writer in Eastern Europe* (Chicago: The University of Chicago Press, 2006).

Wischebart, Rüdiger. "E book 2018," interview by Chris Kenneally; online: https://beyondthebookcast.com/wp-content/uploads/2018/12/Wischenbart EBooksAct2Transcript.pdf [accessed 2019-05-10].

Wögerbauer, Michael – Píša, Petr – Šámal, Petr – Janáček, Pavel and co. *V obecném zájmu. Cenzura a sociální regulace literatury v moderní české kultuře 1749–2014. Svazek II (1938–2014)* (Praha: Academia – Institute of Czech Literature, CAS).

Wolf, Maryanne. *Proust and the Squid. The Story and Science of the Reading Brain* (London: Icon Books, 2008 [2007]).

————. *Tales for Literacy fot the 21st Century* (Oxford: Oxford University Press, 2016).

————. *Reader, Come Home. The Reading Brain in a Digital World* (New York: Harper Collins Publishers, 2018).

WOLFF, Katarzyna. *Książka w społecznej przestrzeni polskiej wsi* (Warszawa: Biblioteka Narodowa, 2008).

ZAID, Gabriel. *So Many Books. Reading and Publishing in an Age of Abundance*, transl. by Natascha Wimmer (Philadelphia: Paul Dry Books, 2003).

Zákon o veřejných knihovnách obecních č. 430/1919 Sb. a navazující předpisy; online: https://ipk.nkp.cz/docs/legislativa/KnihovniZakon_1919.doc [accessed 2020-03-31].

zav. "Nakladatelé žádají Babiše o pomoc. Varují před likvidací knižního trhu"; *iDNES* (25. 3. 2020); online: https://www.idnes.cz/kultura/literatura /nakladatele-knizni-trh-vyzva-premier-andrej- babis.A200325_112029_literatura _kiz [accessed 2020-04-02].

Zpráva o českém knižním trhu 2018/2019; online: fhttps://www.sckn.cz/file /wysiwyg/files/Zprava_o_ceskem_kniznim_trhu_2018_19.pdf [accessed 2020-04-02].

Online addresses (websites)

http://bettymacdonaldfanclub.blogspot.cz/

https://bisg.org/page/research

http://www.eblida.org/activities/kic/public-libraries-statistics.html

https://www.czso.cz

https://ereadcost.eu/

https://www.euread.com/

https://ec.europa.eu/eurostat/data/database

https://fep-fee.eu/

https://geediting.com/world-reading-habits-2018/

https://www.ibisworld.com/global/market-research-reports/global-book -publishing-industry/

https://www.ifla.org/

https://www.internationalpublishers.org/

https://ourworldindata.org/literacy

https://www.statista.com/statistics/288746/global-book-market-by-region/

https://www.sckn.cz/

https://www.stiftunglesen.de/

https://thenewpublishingstandard.com/category/the-global-book-market/

https://www.wischenbart.com/

Appendices

Appendix 1 Statistical surveys of the population aged 15 + (2007, 2010, 2013, 2018) – technical parameters

basic characteristics	2007	2010	2013	2018
character of research	representative	representative	representative	representative
agency	DEMA	DEMA	ppm factum	Nielsen Admosphere
nature of research	quantitative	quantitative	quantitative	quantitative
population	CR 15+	CR 15+	CR 15+t	CR 15+
sample	1, 551 respondents	1,550 respondents	1 ,584 respondents	2,007 respondents
mean statistical error	2.5%	2.5%	2.5%	2.0%
locality	Czech Republic, all regions	Czech Republic, all regions	Czech Republic, all regions	Czech Republic, all regions
selection method	quota	quota	quota	quota
data collection method	standardized face-to-face interviews	standardized face-to-face interviews	standardized face-to-face interviews	online collection (CAWI)
form of questions	closed, half-closed, open	closed, half-closed, open	closed, half-closed, open	closed, half-closed, open
implementation of data collection	25 May – 16 June 2007	1–30 June 2010	2-25 May 2013	11 May – 18 June 2018

Appendix 2   Statistical surveys of the child population (2013/2014 and 2017) – technical parameters

basic characteristics	2013/2014	2017
character of research	representative	representative
agency	Nielsen Admosphere	Nielsen Admosphere
nature of research	quantitative and qualitative	quantitative and qualitative
sample	children CR 6-14	children and youth CR 6-19
population	513 younger children aged 6-8 and 1,519 older children aged 9-14	504 younger children aged 6-8 and 817 aged 9-14; 688 aged 15-19
mean statistical error	2.0%	2.0%
locality	Czech Republic, all regions	Czech Republic, all regions
selection method	quota	quota
data collection method	standardized face-to-face interviews in the respondents' homes (with parents' written permission)	standardized interviews using the CAPI method in the respondents' homes (with parents' written permission for children up to 15)
form of questions	closed, half-closed, open	closed, half-closed, open
implementation of data collection (quantitative section)	Sep 2013 - May 2014	Sep - Oct 2017
qualitative section	in-depth interviews with child and parents for children aged 6-8 ; *focus groups* (5-7 children) for children aged 9-14	Phase 1-41 individual in-depth interviews with children, their parents and youth aged 6-19; Phase 2 was attended by 85% of respondents from Phase 1

Appendix 3 Reading life stories

reading life stories (clues and keywords)

	childhood	youth	adulthood	seniorhood
required	- family background (parents: descent, profession) - parents reading out loud - what reading was like at home - first contact with a book - home library	- knowledge of reading before school - acquisition of reading skills - school and its influence (teachers, classmates) - reading diaries - classmates, friends - parents' influence - "my first adult book" - forbidden books - school and public libraries - other media and their influence	- reading and one's own family (partner, children) - buying books - reading and employment - reading and leisure time - weakening and revitalization - reading and other media	- retirement: return to books and reading - illnesses and indispositions - reading and other media in final conclusion: my favourite author, favourite book and the book I keep coming back to; readers' habits and rituals; other media – how much of each
possible	fairy tales, pop-up picture books, book illustrations, rivalry between television, internet and books; the first book I read	"compulsory" reading, buying books, the generational barrier, resistance to reading, literature for boys and girls	I've completely stopped reading, book buying, libraries, the book that helped me deal with a difficult situation in life	reading for grandchildren, returning to libraries, the books I go back to, inability to read current output, the view of the younger generation, readers' (lifelong) habits and stereotypes; a retrospective view, what I would do differently.
individual basis (based on the temperaments and dispositions of the narrators)	here it is now possible to give space to interviewees for their own inclinations, e.g. where they face a particularly important individual such as a prominent teacher, the parental model, the strong influence of the library, the initiation into reading experience, a strong barrier and distinctive reading and anti-reading statements etc.			

Appendix 4 Favourite books in a Czech TV survey: The Book of my Heart (2009)*

	title	votes
1.	*Saturnin* - Zdeněk Jirotka	38 430
2.	*Babička* (Granny) - Božena Němcová	29 935
3.	*Le Petit Prince* (The Little Prince) - Antoine de Saint-Exupéry	24 232
4.	*Twilight* - Stephenie Meyer	24 217
5.	*Harry Potter* - Joanne K. Rowling**	22 665
6.	*Sinuhe egyptiläinen* (The Egyptian) - Mika Waltari	19 674
7.	*Alla vi barn i Bullerbyn* (The Six Bullerby Children) - Astrid Lindgren	14 245
8.	*Anybody Can Do Anything, The Plague and I, Onion in the Stew* trilogy - Betty MacDonald	13 348
9.	*The Lord of the Rings* - J. R. R. Tolkien	12 941
10.	*Osudy dobrého vojáka Švejka za světové války* (The Good Soldier Švejk) - Jaroslav Hašek	10 362
11.	*Rychlé šípy* (Rapid Arrows) - Jaroslav Foglar	9 731
12.	*O Alquimista* (The Alchemist) - Paulo Coelho	6 742
13.	*The Egg and I* (Betty MacDonald)	3 373
14.	*The Chronicles of Narnia* (C. S. Lewis)	1 996
15.	*Bylo nás pět* (There Were Five of Us) - Karel Poláček	1 989

* a total of 322,881 readers voted, ** entire series and parts

Source: Czech TV

Appendix 5 Favourite books based on statistical representative research (2018)

	title	mentions
1.	Harry Potter (Joanne K. Rowling)	16
2.	The Good Soldier Švejk (Jaroslav Hašek)	10
3.	The Egg and I (Betty MacDonald)	9
4.	Winnetou (Karl May)	9
5.	Fifty Shades of Grey (Erika L. James)	9
6.	Lord of the Rings (John Ronald Reuel Tolkien)	8
7.	The Witcher (Andrzej Sapkowski)	6
8.	The Egyptian (Mika Waltari)	6
9.	The Snowman (Jo Nesbø)	5
10.	Saturnin (Zdeněk Jirotka)	5

Source: Czech National Library – Institute of Czech Literature, CAS

Appendix 6. Favourite authors based on a statistical representative survey (2018)

	author	mentions
1.	Jo Nesbø	28
2.	Michal Viewegh	18
3.-4.	Danielle Steel	17
3.-4.	Agatha Christie	17
5.	Joanne K. Rowling	11
6.-8.	Stephen King	10
6.-8.	John Ronald Reuel Tolkien	10
6.-8.	Dick Francis	10
9.-12.	Erich Maria Remarque	9
9.-12.	Lenka Lanczová	9
9.-12.	Jaroslav Foglar	9
9.-12.	Patrik Hartl	9

Source: Czech National Library – Institute of Czech Literature, CAS

Appendix 7 Largest Czech publishers

	name	titles 2018	titles 2019
1.	Albatros Media (Prague)	1,505	1,563
2.	Euromedia Group (Prague)	775	828
3.	Moravská Bastei - MOBA (Brno)	373	343
4.	Svojtka & Co. (Prague)	316	183
5.	Grada Publishing (Prague)	296	350
6.	Dobrovský (Prague)	245	355
7.	Mladá fronta (Prague)	237	165
8.	Crew (Prague)	212	209
9.	Argo (Prague)	210	234
10.	Karolinum (Prague)	189	262

Source: Association of Czech Booksellers and Publishers

Appendix 8 Czech book market turnover

year	2013	2014	2015	2016	2017	2018	2019
total turnover (CZK billions)	7.2	7.2	7.5	7.8	8.0	8.3	8.6
year-on-year change	0%	0%	+4%	+4%	+2,5%	3,5%	3,5%

Source: Association of Czech Booksellers and Publishers

Appendix 9 Exhibitors and visitors at the World of Book trade fair (Prague)

year	2010	2011	2012	2013	2014	2015
exhibitors	416	322	395	339	409	393
visitors	40,000	38,000	36,000	36,000	38,000	38,000

year	2016	2017	2018	2019	2020*
exhibitors	407	396	404	461	
visitors	42,000	44,000	46,000	51,000	

* cancelled due to coronavirus pandemic

Source: Association of Czech Booksellers and Publishers

Appendix 10   Largest public libraries by collection size (2019)

	name	city	book units
1.	National Library	Prague	7,439,638
2.	Moravian Library in Brno	Brno	4,276,521
3.	Olomouc Research Library	Olomouc	2,308,687
4.	Regional Study and Research Library in Plzeň	Plzeň	1,992,560
5.	Prague Municipal Library	Prague	1,741,574
6.	Hradec Králové Study and Research Library	Hradec Králové	1,443,784
7.	South Bohemian Research Library in České Budějovice	České Budějovice	1,435,269
8.	Regional Research Library in Liberec	Liberec	1,386,348
9.	Moravian-Silesian Research Library in Ostrava	Ostrava	1,231,961
10.	Central Bohemian Research Library in Kladno	Kladno	991,929

Source: Czech National Library

Index